DECODING
LOVE
UNDERSTANDING IS COMPASSION

SHARAM

EDITED BY
SHAHED & NAFISEH

TALIA

DECODING LOVE:
UNDERSTANDING IS COMPASSION
SHARAM

EDITED BY: SHAHED & NAFISEH
PAPERBACK 1ST EDITION
PUBLISHED IN 2014 BY:

TALIA

TALIA, FRIENDS OF EXISTENCE, INC.
WEBSITE: WWW.TALIAFRIENDS.ORG
EMAIL: TALIA@TALIAFRIENDS.ORG

COPYRIGHT © 2014 BY TALIA, FRIENDS OF EXISTENCE, INC.
ISBN 978-0-9839873-3-8

ALL RIGHTS RESERVED.

NO PART OF THIS BOOK MAY BE REPRODUCED, STORED IN A RETRIEVAL SYSTEM, OR TRANSMITTED IN ANY FORM OR BY ANY MEANS, ELECTRONIC, MECHANICAL, PHOTOCOPYING, RECORDING OR OTHERWISE, WITHOUT THE PRIOR WRITTEN PERMISSION OF THE PUBLISHER.

MANY THANKS TO MELINA H & STEFAN HOELSCHER FOR THEIR INVALUABLE HELP.
COVER ART: SHARAM
COVER DESIGN & PAGE LAYOUT: NO MIND DESIGN

IN APPRECIATION OF THEIR
INVALUABLE SUPPORT,
THIS BOOK IS DEDICATED TO
STEFAN HOELSCHER AND
DR. RANDY WRIGHT.

*Mysticism is not about sitting there
and saying Ommmmmm....
It's about understanding ourselves,
which is very exciting and fun.
The best thing in the whole world
is to understand.
Nothing comes close to it.
That's what I call mysticism.*

— SHARAM —

TABLE OF CONTENTS

INTRODUCTION *xi*
WATER IS A MIRACLE *1*
SPACE: THE FINAL FRONTIER *2*
SPIRITUAL HOMEWORK *6*
THE LAWS OF NATURE AND THE LAWS OF THE BEYOND *8*
TO ERR IS NOT ONLY HUMAN, IT'S ESSENTIAL *10*
USE IT, DON'T MISUSE IT! *13*
INSISTING AND DOUBTING *14*
THE BASEMENT OF OUR SOUL *15*
LIFE IS GOOD *17*
NO CHOICE IS THE RIGHT CHOICE *19*
TRUST … AND THE BEYOND WILL BE WITH YOU *20*
TRICK OF THE EGO *24*
SNEAKY PETE *25*
AWARENESS AND INTELLIGENCE *26*
INTELLIGENCE OF THE EGO *27*
FASCINATING! *29*
SUFFERING SUCCOTASH! *30*
STUPIDITY IS WHAT YOU "THINK" *31*
COMPARISON: THE MAIN ARTERY OF THE EGO *33*
MAKE IT SIMPLE *35*
COMPARISON: A DIRECT ROUTE TO HELL *37*
EGO, BIG OR SMALL *39*
MOMS, DADS AND THE COURAGE TO EXPRESS OURSELVES *40*
PRIDE *42*

Breathe More Deeply   44
You Are Who You Are,
Which Is Exactly Who You Are Supposed To Be   46
Drinking from a Mirage   47
I Don't Exist   48
Coming Off the "I Don't Exist" Exercise   50
Perfect Harmony   52
Love Them Anyway   53
Hell   55
Love Is Giving Them Hell   56
Getting Insulted   57
Fear: Fresh Lemonade for the Soul   60
Caution: Do Not Wash in Worry
Shrinkage Will Occur!   63
Hiding   64
Withdrawing   65
Fear of the Unknown   68
Laugh It Out   70
Express Your Way to a Beautiful Life   72
The Secret of Expression   73
Peacemaker   75
The Key to Your Soul   77
Tension in the Line   80
Like a Weed   83
God: The Empty Space between Your Ears   84
Old Patterns   86
Old Couples   89
Wisdom of Hate   90
Being Special   91
The Sounds of Ego   93
I Want To Like Myself   95

CRITICISM IS HARD TO ACCEPT   97
LIKING YOURSELF AND OTHERS   98
THE BENEFITS OF NOT LIKING YOURSELF   101
WHAT COLOR'S YOUR CARPET?   103
PATIENCE: THE PATH TO KINDNESS   107
TICK-TOCK   109
THE FOUNTAIN OF LIFE   111
MESSAGES FROM THE PAST   112
WHERE IS THE LOVE?   114
EVERYBODY IS HIGH   115
DON'T GIVE IN TO THE EGO   116
THE SCHOOL OF LIFE   117
UNDERSTANDING:
THE BRIDGE BETWEEN FAITH AND AWARENESS   119
BE AWARE: AWARENESS IS COMING   121
THE DEEPER THE ISSUE,
THE LONGER IT TAKES—SOMETIMES   123
H-ANGRY   125
MOODS OF THE MOON   127
KUNDALINI AND DEATH   129
WHY LAY OVER WHEN YOU CAN GO DIRECT?   131
RESPECT & POWER:
NOT ALL THEY'RE CRACKED UP TO BE   133
THE PATH OF MEDITATION   136
I DON'T GET IT   138
GOOD JOB   139
DO NOTHING   141
MOTIVATION   142
MORNINGS, MIND, AND MEDITATION   144
MY MOTHER'S APPROVAL   145
FEELING EMPTY   146
THE ILLUSION OF LACK   149

Balancing Money 152
Break It To Make It 153
Appreciation
Just Do It! 156
The First Chakra 157
The Second Chakra and Its Desire To Dominate 158
Loneliness 159
You Can't Fix It If You Ain't Got the Tools 160
Anger 162
Sex and the Chakras 163
Jealousy 164
A Mystic's Job 166
Money, Work, and a Big Ego 167
Dreams and Chakras 169
Enlightenment Is Easy 170
The Great Opportunity 172
Mind: The Great Defender 173
Cunning Mind 175
Giving Space 178
Blowing Things out of Proportion 180
Spilled Milk 182
Forget It! 185
My Own Creation 186
Blame 188
Blame Me, Please 189
The Eternal Lightness of Nastiness 190
What Goes Around Comes Around—
A Complicated Matter 192
Resistance and Fight 194
You *Can* Stop Their Anger 195
The Secret of Love 197

Beauty and the Beast   200
The Subtle Love of Existence   201
Free Inside and Out   202
Get Out Your Fly Swatters and Let's Go A-Swattin'   204
A Wake Up Call   206
Guilt Buster   208
Let Existence Be Your Judge   209
From Nowhere to Nowhere   211
Balance Is a Moment-to-Moment Thing   213
Tricks of the Negative Mind   215
Breaking Faith   216

*Anytime we get upset,
right away we say,
"What is wrong with these people?"
We never say,
"What is wrong with me
that I get upset so easily?"*

∾ SHARAM ∾

INTRODUCTION

OFTEN UNDERSTANDING OURSELVES in relation to others and to our experiences can be a complicated process. As they say, it is always easier to see the other guy's strengths and weaknesses than our own. We hear things like the importance of being in the moment, but the experience of it escapes us. Or our parents or pastors have told us to love your neighbor as you love yourself, but when we are standing face to face with a red-faced angry neighbor as he chews us out over some ridiculous thing like our lawn being too long, when his dogs haven't stopped barking since the day he moved in, we think, "Hey, if you want to love him, feel free, but I'm not giving him the time of day." We feel justified in our dislike of the guy and we spend a lot of time and energy reinforcing this dislike, but in the end, where does it get us? Do we feel energized and happy every time we bump into each other? Do we feel joyful, free and ecstatic? No, but how do we get the motivation to look at our part in this whole nightmare? I mean come on, look at the guy.

In *Decoding Love*, Sharam, in speaking with his students, demonstrates over and over again how *our* egos (not the neighbor) cause us misery and suffering, how we choose misery time after time by resisting or not liking ourselves, others, or what is happening around us. Resistance can mean anything from fighting with your neighbor to not fully listening to the person talking to you because you are thinking about what you need to do next, or getting frustrated because the barista got the foam wrong on your venti, non-fat, no foam, extra hot chai tea latte. We resist rather than trusting in the perfection of Existence.

In talking with people, Sharam goes deeper into the experiences of their lives and shows them the love in all that happens. But the love of Existence doesn't necessarily look like the image we have of love in our minds. Existence wants us to grow. What does that mean? Simply put, it means to lessen the grip of our ego upon us, and ultimately to shed the ego altogether. This love can take the form of kindness or hardship—whatever it takes to help us wake up. Sharam often reminds people that hardship is not punishment: "If you talk with me, you will see that there is no room for punishment in Existence. Existence never wants to punish us; it just wants to remind us of something or make us aware of something. It wants to teach us something. Existence is not about punishment. Existence is all love."

Decoding Love gives beautiful examples of the power of deeper understanding in increasing love and acceptance.

Spiritual lessons and understanding of deeper issues need time and space to sink in. So if you feel like you can only read a few pages at a time, that's a very good sign.

WATER IS A MIRACLE

MELINA: What is a miracle?

SHARAM: Just the fact that we are alive is a miracle. All the little subtle things that happen all day long to save us from harm, they are all miracles. Love is a miracle. Laughter is a miracle. Water is a miracle. Imagine if there was no water, we would not be alive. The Earth would be one big desert, no life. Food is a miracle. Everything there is is a miracle. We have not created any of these. They are made by Existence. If I do a beautiful painting, even that is a miracle. How can I create such a thing? It comes from the Beyond. Just the fact that I am alive and can do the painting is a miracle. In fact, there are no miracles, because life is happening by itself. We only call some parts of life miraculous; those that are out of ordinary or beyond what we can understand, beyond what we ordinarily see.

SPACE:
THE FINAL FRONTIER

MAYA: I see that sometimes it is hard for me to be with someone, but other people spend time with them just fine. Then I realize it must be something wrong with me. Can you help me please to see it?

SHARAM: That's because you don't give space to people.

MAYA: Why don't I give space to others?

SHARAM: Because you didn't have space growing up, so you think, "They don't deserve space."

MAYA: But I see people that had space growing up and they also don't give space sometimes.

SHARAM: It is impossible. Maybe that person had space growing up from their father, but not from the mother. If your mother doesn't give you space, then it's really hard for you to give space to others.

MAYA: I see I didn't have space growing up, so I don't know how to give space. What do I do now?

SHARAM: You have to learn it.

MAYA: How do I do that?

SHARAM: With bringing understanding. Like right now, you compared yourself to others and you realized that you don't give space. This is the way: compare, witness, and understand.

MAYA: You know, I feel that if I am nice and supportive to someone that I don't like to be with, it feeds my ego because I think I am better than them. I just want to support them and feel good about myself.

SHARAM: It doesn't matter; you are still giving space regardless of who they are. That has its own positivity.

MAYA: If someone is older than me, it's harder for me to give them space, but if they are younger, it is easier.

SHARAM: You are discriminating by age. It doesn't matter how old the person is; everyone needs love and space. And when you don't give them love and space, they don't grow.

MAYA: *(laughter)* So it's my fault that they don't grow?

SHARAM: Yes, exactly. You got it right! They feel that they are not loved because you and people like you don't give them space.

MAYA: If they are not lovable, why don't they do something to become lovable? If I want people to love me, I do something about it.

SHARAM: This is being tough. You cannot compare them to yourself. Maybe you had a different upbringing, maybe you were brought up in a different society; a thousand and one things could be different for them. Maybe they didn't have the privileges you had. How can they learn anything? Learning should come by and by with love and space.

MAYA: Wow! This is so different from what they teach us in society. In society everything is like school. The teacher is tough on students, so they will learn something.

SHARAM: Yes, that's true. But here in the school of mysticism we give love and space to people, as much as they need, so they can grow.

MAYA: So what does love mean and how do we give love?

SHARAM: Love means to make the space softer. Everybody needs love. Everyone is after love and *you* enjoy when you give love. Love means letting the energy of Existence to come in.

MAYA: When I want to give love to someone and not to another person, what does it mean?

SHARAM: It means that you are selfish. You want to give love to someone who gives it back to you. If someone doesn't know how to return your love, you don't want to give them love. You are discriminating. This is not love anymore. It's more like business. Sometimes you see people say, "Look I gave her two presents and she only gave me one." This person has problems with the first chakra, money and things. With you it is more about relationship, emotions, and respect. You say, "I said hello to them three times and they only said hello one time!"

MAYA: *(laughter)* It's very true. I think about how nice I am to them and still they are nasty!"

SHARAM: But if you don't care what they do, you give them love anyway. Then you enjoy. You understand that this is their personality, to be angry and grumpy, and your personality is to be nice. You do your part and enjoy. In that environment, anyone would change. If they are not changing it is because we are not giving them enough love. Everyone needs love to grow. If you love them, they grow.

*If you love, you love.
It makes no difference if the other is
a friend or an enemy.*

∽ SHARAM ∽

SPIRITUAL HOMEWORK

Melina told a story of a situation she was in and then she asked:

MELINA: If someone says something to me with negativity, I don't like it. Why is that?

SHARAM: Because they bring their ego in and nobody likes ego.

MELINA: So what is my part in this?

SHARAM: I am giving you a break by saying that is their fault! *(Laughter)*

MELINA: And if I don't want the break, then what?

SHARAM: Okay, let's not give you a break. They have their ego. If we don't want a break, and we want to go higher, we should accept that people have egos and it is fine. I don't say to like their ego, I'm just saying to be okay with it. Just see that they have an ego and their ego likes to criticize you. You can't do anything about it, so why should you bother yourself over it? It is not worth it. The guy is a jerk and that's okay.

MELINA: But you always say that we have a part in everything that happens.

SHARAM: There are always two possibilities to every situation: one is like homework from Existence for us and the other is an opportunity for us to look and see our part in that situation. This situation was homework for you. The homework was for you to see or to recognize that this is their ego and it's okay. You got hurt by it and that's okay too; but if it is their ego why should you get upset? In general there are different scenarios from lower to higher: We say,

1. That's their ego. Shame on them. I never want to see them again.
2. It's their ego, and my ego has got hurt by it and that's okay.
3. It's their ego and it's okay. They can be whoever they want to be.
4. What just happened was a test for me. Existence is helping me to grow. This is my homework to see how I react to them.
5. The higher is that enlightenment is there and I don't have homework anymore. This is the way people are and I love them the way they are. What a beautiful ego!

Only with acceptance can you go beyond.
My message all the time is:
acceptance takes you to the Beyond,
beyond the problems,
whatever they are.
That's the punch line in life.

∾ SHARAM ∾

THE LAWS OF NATURE AND THE LAWS OF THE BEYOND

SHARAM: There are two kinds of laws, the laws of nature and the laws of super-nature *(or the Beyond)*. The laws of the Beyond overrule the laws of nature. If you bring understanding, then you can break the laws of nature. For example, if someone gets mad at you, you get mad back at them automatically; that is the law of nature. But with understanding, with the law of the Beyond, you have the option to get angry or not. It is your choice. When you have higher understanding and awareness, you can choose to fall into that game or not and that is the breaking of the laws of nature.

*Awareness breaks all the rules.
It changes everything.
That's why we emphasize awareness here.
Love has the same effect.
It also breaks all the rules.
Love brings awareness because it is total.
When there is totality,
there is awareness.*

— SHARAM —

TO ERR IS NOT ONLY HUMAN, IT'S ESSENTIAL

RABIA: I keep messing everything up.

SHARAM: Messing up is part of creativity.

RABIA: I just want to get conscious enough to quit messing everything up.

SHARAM: That would be the day you die, because people who don't mess up are dead people. Machines don't mess up, but humans make mistakes. That's the most beautiful trait of human beings. It's a necessary part of creativity. Making mistakes really doesn't exist, but since you insist, it means making things alive.

RABIA: But people around me don't mess anything up. It's only me and they are really growing.

SHARAM: If they don't mess anything up, that growth is phony. Yes, they are growing but it is their ego that is growing. And if their ego grows, they become more and more the enemy of Existence. On the surface maybe it looks like they have it all together, but inside the ego is making them suffer.

RABIA: But they keep getting blessings.

SHARAM: What kind of blessing is it when they don't get to see their ego? They hide it and hide it and hide it. On the surface they look like they are so blessed and great, but they are just hiding a lot of negativity inside. People who mess things up are the most beautiful people on Earth. People who never make mistakes are machines, and they get big egos.

Machines are beautiful; they don't have egos. They don't make mistakes, but they don't get big egos either. Human beings that never make mistakes get big egos. They are really damaging themselves. That is not the way of mysticism. The way of mysticism is to mess things up, so your ego doesn't get big. The whole of mysticism is all about doing something so the ego doesn't get big. Existence loves you so much that it helps you make mistakes. Existence loves everyone. If it doesn't help some people to make mistakes, that is also for a higher reason. Maybe these people cannot see their ego as it is, so they need to make it bigger to see it.

RABIA: Maybe people get past having to make mistakes.

SHARAM: There is no such thing as getting past making mistakes. I make mistakes all the time.

RABIA: You never make a mistake.

SHARAM: Then you don't know. I mess things up all the time. But when we look deeper even this isn't true. Everyone thinks *they* are making a mistake, but how can that be if Existence runs the show? We are conditioned that certain things are bad. If we do those bad things then we call it a mistake. If you go to the roots and look at it deeper, there is no such a thing as making a mistake. We have been conditioned that certain things are good and certain things are bad. There is wisdom in that. When there is good and bad, then there is the opportunity to make mistakes, which keeps our egos from growing. You think you have messed up and you are not perfect, just so your ego doesn't get bigger. That is the wisdom. Really, there are no mistakes because that is like saying God is messing up. It just doesn't happen. You make mistakes because you really don't want to mess up your life.

RABIA: So you mess up because you don't want to mess up your life. If you don't mess things up, then you really mess up your life. But shouldn't we learn something from our mistakes?

SHARAM: You don't need to learn anything from your mistakes; the point is that your ego has not gotten bigger. That's the only thing; it is not about learning.

RABIA: What if other people get hurt in the process?

SHARAM: If other people get hurt, Existence wanted them to get hurt, so that they can move forward. Anyone who gets stuck somewhere will get hurt. Hurt means moving forward. It means pushing them to move forward. Existence is using you to help them. God bless you; you are doing the job of Existence. You are the hand of Existence helping yourself and others. You see how beautiful that is? Again, Existence is 180 degrees opposite from what we believe and think. We are constantly looking at the ways in which the laws of Existence are 180 degrees opposite from what they teach us in society. Of course we should not walk around hurting people and say God wants this.

USE IT, DON'T MISUSE IT!

SHARAM: There was a discussion about some money issue. Shahed made a comment and I showed her the limitation of her mind. She said something very interesting: "I have two parts inside of me. One part feels or says something and my other part that is spiritual condemns it. This is what was happening right now. My spiritual part was putting down my other part."

SHARAM: See that you are using mysticism to put yourself down, to judge yourself. This is not the purpose of mysticism. Mysticism is there for gaining higher understanding, not for condemnation. This is not the function of the path. Don't use it to put yourself or others down, use it to pull yourself up.

INSISTING AND DOUBTING

Jesse insists that she has to do six hours of meditation every day. When Sharam tells her to do less, she objects. At one point she asked:

JESSE: Is it effective to do the six hours?

SHARAM: You have two parts inside of you and they don't agree with each other. One part says this is good for you, and the other part does not want to do it. What you are really saying is that you don't want to do six hours. For the past year, you have insisted that you should do six hours of meditation, but unconsciously, you didn't want to do it. That's why you are not total in your meditation, and that's why it doesn't work.

THE BASEMENT OF OUR SOUL

SHARAM: One of my students told me she came out of her house and her car was stolen. I said to her, "Congratulations. You did a good job." She said, "What? I didn't do anything. The car was stolen." I told her, "You created it. You did it. The car was old. You didn't want it. You wanted a new one. Unless the old goes away, how can you get the new?" She created this from the unconscious. She asked me, "What is the unconscious?" I told her the unconscious is two things. First, it has the negative part, which sits in the etheric body. The etheric body is a layer of the soul that starts in your spine and extends just a little outside the body, all around the body. This is your basement, the place where you throw all your unwanted negativity, the negative things that you hide and then it becomes unconscious. Beyond the etheric body, there are several other layers (bodies) that surround the physical body and stretch outside of this room. We are not conscious of these either, so they are also part of our unconscious. The Beyond, or God, is your unconscious too. So the layer which is very close to your body is where all the negativity comes and piles up. All the stuff that you don't want, you throw it here, in the basement of your soul, the first layer. The other layers get closer and closer to the seventh body beyond which is only God. All this is your unconscious.

LIVIA: What is the difference between the subconscious and the unconscious?

SHARAM: There is not much difference. The subconscious is closer to the conscious. The unconscious is deeper. Actually, conscious, subconscious, unconscious, all these are man-made. God didn't make these. I want to make my own definition. Since I am free to call it anything I like, I will drop the subconscious. There is the conscious and the unconscious. The unconscious has two parts—the first layer, which is negative, and beyond that, which is all Existence.

The mind is the conscious part of us and in the mind we can be either positive or negative. What is transformation or growth? That is when we go beyond the positive and negative of the mind with deeper understanding and love. Transformation is when we experience the Beyond. And what is the Beyond? It is all the layers beyond the etheric body (that basement full of negativity). The Beyond is where Existence is.

Don't worry that you don't have a subconscious anymore. It will work *(smiles)*. You will still become enlightened. You will see that it is actually going to help you to get away from too much mind.

LIFE IS GOOD

MONA: I am disappointed with life.

SHARAM: When you don't trust, you don't like your life anymore because you think everybody is your enemy. The only way we find life attractive is for us to feel loved by others. Anytime you feel Existence loves you and is on your side, you feel hopeful and your life works. When you are not trusting, life becomes full of problems and can fall apart in an instant.

MONA: Why don't we trust?

SHARAM: Because in the unconscious, we want to take advantage of others; that's why we think others want to take advantage of us. When you are more conscious, when you are not so much in the ego or the "I," you see that nobody wants to take advantage of you. You trust and you feel warmth in your heart. When you become more aware, love is there. But when you become unaware and something bothers you, your heart closes. You say, "Poor me: see what these people are doing to me."

MONA: So what should I do because my heart is closed mostly?

SHARAM: You've never looked at this so clearly. Now that you are clearer, the next time your heart closes, you'll remember the understanding of today. You'll remember that when your heart closes, you fall into the negative, the mistrusting, and there is no growth there. If you want to grow, you need to go to the positive, because that's where the growth happens. And this awareness helps to take you there. And when you grow, your life has meaning. Growth really means bringing meaning to your life.

NO CHOICE IS THE RIGHT CHOICE

CHRIS: I feel like I am always making the wrong choices.

SHARAM: Choosing is wrong. Yes. Every time you choose, it will be the wrong thing. Ego is wrong, but we have it. Choosing is part of the ego. Yes, it is wrong. Being down here *(living only from the lower chakras)* is wrong. You have to be on top of the mountain *(in the higher chakras, one with Existence)*. We are working our way to get there. Meanwhile we are in the wrong, but that is okay. Not to be enlightened is wrong. You are not enlightened, so you are wrong, but that is okay. Our whole purpose is working towards becoming enlightened. Wrong is okay. Everything that is, is okay.

TRUST
AND THE BEYOND WILL BE WITH YOU

SHAHED: When my husband or sons are struggling, if I make suggestions, they mostly get angry with me and tell me I am not helping. To me they seem like reasonable suggestions, but they want nothing to do with it. My husband gets so angry that I start to feel like I don't have a voice any more, like I can't have an opinion. I end up either feeling very angry or very depressed. I see that I put all my trust in him, in his ability to think clearly, but lately, because of his stubbornness, I am losing trust in him. I need to find that trust in myself, but it just isn't there. I put all my trust in someone else because I don't have any myself.

SHARAM: We had a lesson a few days ago about when there is doubt, there is also no-doubt. I say no-doubt instead of trust, because trust is beyond these poles. The lesson was that if there is doubt, there will be no-doubt. I don't want to say trust because trust is above these poles. The nature of trust is such that you don't put trust in anyone else. There is just trust. You said it so beautifully a minute ago. You said trust is not from outside. It is from inside. When we have trust, we bring an element of the Beyond in, and with the Beyond everything goes well. All of a sudden, everyone around us is fine, everyone is happy, because the beyond comes in. With doubt, we are always in this loop of jumping from one extreme to the other. The Beyond cannot come in; it is not available to us. We put up a barrier to the beyond.

With trust, nothing will disturb us. Nothing will go wrong around us. And even if your sons or your husband are struggling, the Beyond will send some message for them. You say something and all of a sudden they come to their senses. They understand something. Like just right now. You were upset and now the beyond is talking to you through me, because I totally trust Existence. I don't have the opposites. The same thing will happen for you. When you have the element of the Beyond with you, then Existence is there doing incredible things.

So you were right when you said you don't have trust, because if you had trust, it wouldn't be about your husband anymore. It is just Existence and you. Imagine what an amazing, beautiful space it becomes when we have trust. Really anyone, the husband, the wife, the kids, friends, neighbors, fellow travelers in mysticism, it doesn't matter where *they* are. It just matters where *we* are.

SHAHED: If I am continually making people angry, then I am doing something that is making them angry.

SHARAM: Remember, when trust is there, no one gets angry, so we have to learn how to bring in trust *all* the time. We have to go beyond the two opposite poles. Existence is pushing you to do that. Existence is saying, "Come on girl. We have to do it now."

SHAHED: I don't know how to do it. All I'm feeling right now is fear.

SHARAM: When there is trust, there is no fear. When you are in the two opposite poles, then there is fear. Fear is what takes you from one pole to the other. The thing that moves between two opposite poles is fear. When you go to the beyond, there is no fear.

Do you know why trust doesn't need fear? Because fear pushes you from one pole to another. In trust there are no poles. So there is no force to push you around, because you are in oneness. You don't need fear. It is amazing that fear is the force that takes you from doubt to no-doubt, then from no-doubt to doubt. From dislike to like; when you want to go back to dislike, you have to have fear. Fear moves you between the two opposite poles. When you go to the Beyond, there aren't any opposites. You don't need fear. The fear goes away.

Why do we go to the two poles? To make a jump, to go to the Beyond. It is a growth process. Fear is helping us to grow. Now you have come to this fine line. How can I find trust? How can I have Existence on my side? If we want to have Existence on our side, we have to be on the side of Existence. We need that fear. We need to grow. That's why we have fear. That's why we get into these troubles. You are not separate from Existence. You are one with it. Your soul is creating these problems at home to make it really clear that you have to do the jump. We need Existence on our side, and we need to be on the side of Existence.

SHAHED: I feel I get on the side of Existence for a little while. I become centered and feel that everything will be okay, but then my husband starts talking fear in his sleep; he is talking fear out loud, and then I can't breathe. You always tell me I'll have enough money, but my husband is telling me, "No. We can't buy anything right now."

SHARAM: This is the sound of Existence talking to you. "You can't buy anything. You can't do anything." It is trying to tell you not to do anything. Just be. It is the force of Existence in the voice of your husband. This is the time for you, finally, not to do anything and learn how to just be. Not to buy anything and learn how to be. Wow. I hear the voice of God in the mouth of your husband. If we just look at it in the right way—that Existence is telling you that life is not about doing and buying, life is about being. So he is telling you to just be. You don't hear that. You just panic.

SHAHED: I *try* to hear it. It comes and goes.

SHARAM: You said something very beautiful. You said there are times when you become centered, very much centered. I want to pick up from there. Fear takes you from one pole to another, and then, you do the jump to centeredness. You go higher. You grow. Then again from there, quickly, you move into fear again. You go to the opposite place, because your soul knows that life is short. We have to get to a very concrete place—enlightenment—where everything makes sense. Pure clarity. To get there we have to continue to grow, so you don't stay in the centeredness long. If we stay there for more than a few hours, it becomes worthless, so you quickly start doing your thing. Fear, fear, fear, fear, centeredness, fear, fear, fear, fear, centeredness. You keep advancing. I see it in you. Your soul is directing you immensely, beautifully.

So, there is unconscious work going on here, without you being aware of it. Where does this unconscious come from? It comes from the soul, the Beyond. We are not conscious of the layers of our soul, but they are also at work. They are doing something. You have been working on these layers, when we do meditation, when I work with you, like right now. That soul is doing its job—creating fear, moving between two opposite poles, and then coming to the center. It is handling the situation so well. I am so glad I said all this to you today. Every time you become centered, things work perfectly. But then you lose it right away because you just want to go higher. The soul knows better.

TRICK OF THE EGO

JESSE: I have not grown at all. Why is that?

SHARAM: Because you fight with everyone all the time.

JESSE: Who do I fight with?

SHARAM: With your husband, with your mother, with me.

JESSE: But I have not fought with you for a long time. It was six months ago that I fought with you. I am not like that anymore.

SHARAM: It is very interesting. You just said that you have not grown at all, but now I say you fight with people and you say I am not like that anymore. So you *have* grown, right? This is the trick of the ego. I just caught your ego deceiving you.

SNEAKY PETE

KATE: The ego does everything not to die, not to let go of its hold on us. How can we separate ourselves from it?

SHARAM: Ego is intelligence. That's why the ego is so tricky. The more subtle your ego, the more intelligence you have. Ego is the mind. How can we separate ourselves from the mind? By watching, by paying attention. Watching destroys the mind, the ego. Watching is an ego destroyer. It separates us from the mind, the body, and the emotions. Paying attention to these three is the way to freedom from the ego.

AWARENESS AND INTELLIGENCE

MAYA: What is the difference between awareness and intelligence?

SHARAM: Intelligence is from the ego and awareness is from the soul. Intelligence is there to notice things around you, and to be sharp. Awareness is for deep understanding, for looking at things from different angels. With intelligence you have to focus, but with awareness you don't focus, instead you look at the whole picture.

MAYA: Is intelligence the same as intellect?

SHARAM: No, intellect is only from the mind. Intelligence is from the ego: it is a collection of the mind and all the emotions, past memories, wounds, grudges, anger, hate, etc. from this lifetime and past lifetimes. Awareness is from the soul.

INTELLIGENCE OF THE EGO

MAYA: My mother is very intelligent, but she is also very harsh. Why is that?

SHARAM: Because intelligence *is* ego. A big ego is intelligent and at the same time, because it is big, it doesn't surrender, it is harsh. The West is all about intelligence, big egos and non-surrendering. That's why life has become meaningless. The East has surrender, but no intelligence. A high quality person is someone that is intelligent—has a big ego—but also has enough awareness to surrender his ego. It is hard because people either have small egos, which are easy to surrender, and not much intelligence or they have high intelligence and a big ego, which is harder to surrender. So we can be intelligent, but if we don't surrender our ego, we don't have higher intelligence or wisdom. We just have book smarts.

MAYA: I understand that I needed my mother to get to the path of understanding, but, now that I am on the path, I still have to deal with her harshness. What is the message of Existence for me at this point?

SHARAM: Existence is helping you to learn to not let her put her harshness on you. The more you let her do that, the harsher she becomes.

MAYA: The last time she was harsh, I didn't do anything. I wanted to hang up the phone, but I couldn't because I didn't want to be disrespectful to her. Why is that? Is it because I am weak?

SAHRAM: You didn't have this understanding at that time (to not let her put her harshness on you), and because this path is all about being loving, you didn't do anything. So there is no such a thing as weak or strong. We either have an understanding or not. If we have an understanding and we act upon it, it looks like strength, and if we don't have it then what we do appears as weakness. There are also some people who have a very big ego. They don't give *any* space to others so they look tough or strong, but that is not real strength. Mostly, they feel weak, but they try to hide it by being tough.

FASCINATING!

Talking to Farin:

SHARAM: The things that you say are fascinating. They come from your intuition. You don't use your mind; it comes from deep inside of you. That's why it is so fascinating. It is not interesting, because interesting is very low. Fascinating is much higher than interesting. It is from the soul, the divine. Interesting is about the mind and comes from mind. That's why when you say interesting things, they come from what you've read and you've learned. They are interesting. But when you say things from your soul, the quality is so different.

SUFFERING SUCCOTASH!

MAYA: I have suffered a lot in my life. Why?

SHARAM: Ego means conditionings. There are many different egos because there are a variety of conditionings. The bigger the ego, the more you suffer.

STUPIDITY IS WHAT YOU "THINK"

CHRIS: What does being stupid mean?

SHARAM: Being stupid doesn't mean what we think it means. It doesn't mean anything really. It just depends on how much we are conditioned. Conditioning turns us into a computer, only able to respond to things from what we have been taught or experienced in the past, never from the freshness of the moment. The more conditioning we have, the more our real intelligence is hidden. That's the definition of stupidity—more conditioning. But everyone is conditioned more or less the same, so really, stupid is only a figure of speech. Everyone is as smart or stupid as the next guy. It doesn't mean anything. Someone who reads something and doesn't understand it, and they keep reading and don't understand it, that doesn't mean they are stupid. Their mind is somewhere else. Or something could be hard for them because they don't have the background. That doesn't mean they are stupid. If they gave Einstein's theories to me in formulas, it would look like ants walking on paper. Does that mean I am stupid?

I love you very much, Chris. You are very loving. You do many nice things for everyone here.

CHRIS: But I don't think there is any real love in it. Those things are all ego-based.

SHARAM: You said, "I think." Thinking tells us that. Thinking doesn't see love. What can thinking give you except negativity and hate for others? Stupidity is thinking. Thinking is so stupid. Thinking only takes us to an inner fight. It creates a crowd in the head. You don't feel, you think. Thinking *always* takes you to a place of, "I don't deserve anything. I'm just stupid. I'm no good" or "They are no good. They are stupid. They don't deserve anything." I'm so glad you said, "I think." Everything you do is out of your love. You think you do these things to feel deserving, but that is not it. The mind thinks like that, but it is all out of love. Honest. The ego is the thinker. Ego means the mind, which is made up of our conditionings. Everything you do here is out of love. We just have to look at the mind. The tool for looking at the mind is awareness, which comes from meditation and understanding.

COMPARISON
THE MAIN ARTERY OF THE EGO

CHRIS: What is comparison?

SHARAM: It means that you have a notion in the mind and you bring that notion to a situation. You contaminate the situation by injecting some information from the past into it. Comparison is the best way to bring all the memories and information of the past back in front of you. You cannot be in touch with the moment, which is fresh.

Every time you fall down into misery, it is because you are comparing. This is a fact. We have to notice this fact. First we have to accept that it exists and is okay. The second thing is that it is a lifesaver. You compare and you become miserable. Then you want to work on yourself. The more you work on yourself, the more aware you become and the less comparing you do. You have become wiser. You can see more. You still will compare, but less than before because your awareness has increased.

Comparison makes the "me," the "I," very strong. Comparison is always an "I" opener. It is an "I" intensifier. That's why we feel miserable every time we compare. The "I" becomes very big. The focus on "me" becomes very big. It becomes all about "me." It is great food for the ego when we compare. Every time the ego gets big, you feel miserable.

Comparison is a big one. A lot of negativities stem from comparison. It is a root cause of a lot of problems, like ambition. Let's say you don't know a certain gadget exists. You push a button on it and all of a sudden you are invisible. You didn't know about that gadget before, but let's say now your friend has it. You go into comparison: "Why don't I have that?" Then it becomes a desire. All of a sudden you have a desire, an ambition. You have become ambitious to have that gadget.

Comparison is one of the big roots of the ego. Roots have big arteries and then many small stems come out of the big artery. One of the huge arteries of the roots of the ego is comparison. If we can cut that off, the ego becomes weak, becomes ready to leave. Always, when you are ready to compare, you become miserable. The "I" becomes big. Remember that. Even right now or sometime tomorrow, you will remember this sitting and you might think, "Gee, I still compare, so my ego is huge and I am no good." You are taking a memory and using it to compare and then you are miserable.

Also, when *I* use comparison, it will not take you down to misery. In the hands of the heart and soul, comparison is fine. You don't get stuck in it. The energy is dynamic. You move, you grow from it. But in the hands of the mind, comparison takes you to misery.

MAKE IT SIMPLE

CHRIS: Sometimes I feel so stupid.

SHARAM: Yes, you are stupid because you bring complexity to the work and then you don't get it. Simplicity makes for understanding. Comparison and competition make confusion and misery. If you keep comparing, you won't have understanding. If you make it simple, you *will* have understanding.

CHRIS: I don't have anything simple in me. I am all mind.

SHARAM: The mind does its job, which is to bring complexity in: comparison, competition, "I am better"; it goes on and on and on. The mind doubts, then believes, then doesn't trust—it goes everywhere. Then you get confused and you fall apart, the mind becomes crowded and you think you don't understand. All the negativity comes in and all of a sudden you are not good enough. Then you sit here and we make it very simple. We bring in one simple thing. The crowd comes together, becomes united in the head, and one feels, "Thank God, I can breathe. I am happy." Then again you go away and the mind goes haywire. It goes to ten thousand different places. The crowd gathers. They start throwing rocks at each other. They fight and we suffer. Then we bring it to one point. All these crowds become united. They are happy. They are dancing inside. They all hold hands, they hug each other and we feel at peace. This has been going on for years. Right now, we are uniting this crowd because we want to go beyond the duality of the mind.

We want to go beyond the mind, so how do we do that? We focus on meditation and the understanding we get in these sittings. That is the way to go beyond the mind. The mind can stop. You just have to know that this crowd and confusion is the way it is right now; accept it while focusing on meditation. With meditation, you become more and more distant from this whole thing. I am sitting here. I have distance from your mind. That's why I can look at it and be objective. That's why I can unite the crowd inside your head. You can do the same thing. You can stand here, look at the crowd, and through watching them, they will unite. This is awareness. Gradually we become more aware through meditation, and we can observe, as I am observing your mind, and sharing this.

COMPARISON
A DIRECT ROUTE TO HELL

Talking after a meditation:

SHARAM: With the slightest comparison, we bring ourselves down to the depths of hell. Comparison is surely the way to hell. It takes us to suffering right away. Comparison means using the mind to help the soul, but we need to go directly to the soul to help the soul. The amount of good that the mind can do is so little that it is not worth it. Any comparison is the mind sticking its nose in where it doesn't belong. The mind has been given to us to bring us to mysticism. The suffering the mind creates brings us to the path. When you come to mysticism you have to let go of the mind.

All the meditations are for this very simple thing: to learn not to engage with the mind, to just witness the mind. We say sometimes in meditation, "My mind is working so hard." That's good. It gives you a good, hard opportunity to look at it, but we hate it. We say, "Oh no, my mind was working so hard." So what? It is good. If the mind works a little bit, you *can't* witness it. If the mind works a little bit, it has a different function. It is for you to have fun, to relax. Then when your mind is working really hard, really fast and heavy during the meditation, that also has a function. That is for you to witness. Existence constantly, every step, is telling us what is the best thing in that moment, but we don't know how to listen. If the mind works, jump on it, use the opportunity to watch it. If the mind is slowing down, jump on that too and enjoy. Everything is an opportunity, but we just complain, "My mind was working too much." It was good, but it wasn't *sooo* good." Most of the time you don't even say it, you just think that this was a bad meditation.

EGO, BIG OR SMALL

Melina is fourteen years old.

MELINA: You say that the ego has to become big so we can see it. Should my ego also become big?

SHARAM: No. Your ego doesn't need to become big. The only reason I say that is when a person's awareness is not sharp enough to be able to see their ego, so we have to make it bigger in order for them to see it. But in your case, because you have innocence, you are still sharp enough; you don't need to make your ego big. As people get older, their conditionings get stronger and their awareness gets dulled. It becomes harder for them to see themselves. You should be aware not to become proud of your sharpness, though, or you could lose it. When you become proud of something, the ego takes over; the high quality goes away and the ego will make you suffer. Right now you are sharp enough to catch your ego and that's wonderful. You don't need to make it bigger.

MELINA: Thanks Sharam.

MOMS, DADS AND THE COURAGE TO EXPRESS OURSELVES

Sharam talking to Melina:

SHARAM: If you are courageous and you can express yourself, everyone will like you. The way you were growing up was making you a scared person, a mouse, but I changed that. And the way I did it was by first teaching you reasoning. Because when you have reasoning, you can realize things and do something about them. If you are not courageous, all your life people will hit you on the head *(attack you mentally, emotionally, and sometimes physically)*, and you will have a low quality life. Everyone that comes in contact with you will put you down and you will be very angry inside. You will hold lots of grudges and want to get revenge all the time.

MELINA: You said that our souls get attracted to our parents because we are like them. And our conscious and unconscious also comes from our parents. Can you explain that in my case please?

SHARAM: You are a mixture of your parents. Your male is like your father and your female is like your mother. Because you are a girl, what is outside is like your mother and what is underneath is like your father. You and I have broken that. You have replaced me for your father in your unconscious. You used to have problems with your father. If you are born a woman it automatically means that you have problems with your male side. You don't like it; you have pushed your male down into your unconscious. That's why you became a woman. If you are a man you have problems with the female; that's why you become a man. When you become enlightened, you are neither man nor woman. You won't come back to Earth anymore, because on Earth you can only be a man or a woman.

So your conscious was like your mom. You were not courageous, you didn't want to hear anything, and wanted to show off all the time. All of this is going away by and by. Your unconscious and conscious both are getting in order, more and more every day, with understanding. So this doesn't really apply to you anymore. There was a turning point in you when you started liking your father, when you didn't have problems with him anymore. All that happened because I (Sharam) am a man. Your problems were solved with me because you trusted me. The only reason we are a woman and we don't like men is that we don't trust them. We don't trust the male. You really trusted me completely, and all of a sudden your problems with your father disappeared. The male from your father in your unconscious has left and instead a higher male has come in. That's why you are so kind to your father now. You see, so many things can change with a little bit of trust.

PRIDE

MAYA: What is the main issue that I cannot let go of?

SHARAM: Your only problem is your pride. Pride is always serious; pride is always proud; pride always thinks that I am right and everyone else is wrong.

MAYA: I see that I am proud, but I don't know how not to be.

SHARAM: First, accept the fact that you are proud. Then watch it with this acceptance. Accepting and looking together, makes it happen.

MAYA: I see that pride is really disturbing me. I have to spend so much energy making sure that my respect is intact. It takes so much work. But I'm not sure what will happen to me if the pride isn't there anymore. I am afraid. It feels like if the pride is not there, I'm won't be there either.

SHARAM: It is true. You won't be there. God will be there, not you. We are here to become nothing.

MAYA: I can feel the part where I won't be there anymore but I don't understand the part where God enters.

SHARAM: You just have to trust that becoming nothing is equal to becoming the whole of Existence. We have been saying this for years. All the mystics and the poets have repeated it throughout the centuries. You just need a little more trust. Mysticism and divinity are not only there to be talked about. We have to put it to work, someday.

MAYA: When you tell me something about me, I get really upset, even though I know it's true. Why is that?

SHARAM: You get upset because the ego doesn't want to accept it. Some part of you knows it is true, but the other part that is proud doesn't want to accept it. It doesn't want to lose face. It thinks that what has been said brings shame to you.

MAYA: So my problems stick to me because I don't accept them?

SHARAM: Yes, you have to accept them; and look at them with this acceptance. In order to see your ego, first you have to accept that you have an ego. Acceptance plus watching is equal to awareness, and awareness is equal to dissolving of the ego. When we are aware, there is no ego. I really give a lot of credit to anyone who wants to break their ego. It takes years. One has to get used to working on the self, being on the path, and trusting. But on another level this is also beating around the bush. At some point, after years of working on yourself, you just have to put your ego aside and break your pride.

BREATHE MORE DEEPLY

DEBBY: Acceptance means nothing to me.

SHARAM: We can't accept or reject. The only thing we can do is breathe more deeply and connect with our inner soul, which brings acceptance. We don't really do anything. The mind rejects because it's on the surface. Anything on the surface *is* rejection, basically. And anything deeper, closer to our soul, is acceptance. So when we breathe more deeply, we go to acceptance.

DEBBY: So when we start breathing deeper, acceptance comes. It just happens. That same energy can also go and reject, right?

SHARAM: The same energy is either rejection or acceptance. Yes. If we don't breathe more deeply, then most of the time we resist. We don't like. But we have gotten so used to it that we don't even notice that we are rejecting and resisting and fighting all the time.

DEBBY: So when we reject something, it causes our breathing to become shallower. Is that what you're saying?

SHARAM: Exactly—it's fear, fear makes the breathing shallow.

DEBBY: So when we are relaxed and breathing more deeply, the fear leaves and we go towards acceptance. Then we can come to the moment, right?

SHARAM: Yes our soul is the moment so we go towards it. We go towards awareness, being in the present and joy—all that happens. Yes.

YOU ARE WHO YOU ARE, WHICH IS EXACTLY WHO YOU ARE SUPPOSED TO BE

CHRIS: I feel bad. I don't know how to change what I am and I know that what I am is not very good.

SHARAM: I don't see any trust in this. If you trust Existence, then you are who you are, and that's fine because Existence runs the show. We just have to accept it.

DRINKING FROM A MIRAGE

SHARAM: Why is it, when we think of ourselves, we are not happy? Do you know why?

RABIA: We are separating ourselves from Existence?

SHARAM: Because there is no ourselves. It's just illusion. An illusion doesn't exist and there is no happiness in something that doesn't exist. In reality there is happiness. Every time you are not happy that shows you've been thinking of yourself. You've been in illusion. Every single time. And every time you are happy that shows that you are in reality you're not in illusion. Simple. So if you are not happy, know that right now, you are taking a trip in this illusion. You can call it ego trip. We call it illusion trip.

I DON'T EXIST

RABIA: I am sad all the time. I don't know what to do.

SHARAM: For one week don't say "me" or "I." Forget me, I, myself, any reference to yourself, and see what happens. Don't mention yourself; don't think about "you." There will be only silence, because there is nothing else. You don't exist.

RABIA: It's hard for me to believe that all my problems will go away with one exercise. What's really going on when I don't trust what you tell me?

SHARAM: You are really more intelligent. You want to experiment and find out for youself. You're more advanced, but just try it. You don't exist for one week. Think of everybody else, but don't bring "you" into the equation for one week. When someone is wrapped around themselves so much, they become serious, sad. Their life is hell. They always worry about what other people think about them. If there is no "me," I really don't have anything to worry about. If there is no "I," I don't wrap around myself so much. I'm with everyone else, the trees, wind, day, night. My life becomes playful and beautiful; it becomes the most beautiful life. When you think about yourself, catch yourself and stop it. Say, "There is no me, there are only other people; there is only fresh air...."

Judgment about others usually comes with comparing the self. For this exercise, if there is judgment about other people, that's fine. Go with that, but don't bring yourself into it. Don't say, "I." There is no you! Only for one week, don't bring it in. As soon as you bring in the word "I," you get into trouble. Don't think me, poor me. Mind or ego always boils down to poor me. I am the worst, and then we get sad.

"Mine," don't go there. Life becomes really, really wonderful. Finally—freedom. Freedom of the self. Freedom *from* the self. God bless freedom. That's what you want. You have come here *(to Sharam)* to get this and I am giving it to you for a week. People who have more ego think of themselves all the time. They can't enjoy life; they will be sad and crying all the time. When you think of yourself, there is always sadness. That's the definition of ego *(someone who is sad)* because they always think of themselves. When there is no you, how can you think something is wrong or right? There is no you, so things are just the way things are. This is exciting!

*We often talk of inner freedom as self-realization,
but in reality it is no-self-realization,
because we can only be free
when the idea of a self
steps aside.*

∽ SHARAM ∽

COMING OFF THE "I DON'T EXIST" EXERCISE

RABIA: I'm coming off of a week of the "I don't exist" exercise. It went very well except I didn't do it totally of course. I still talked to people. I felt good not feeling sorry for myself or thinking about me as much, but I'm thinking maybe I didn't really do the "I don't exist."

SHARAM: I see it has been successful. I would like you to keep this up. From this exercise, we have learned that every time we think about "me," we always suffer. Like the movie we watched the other day. The main character saved the world three times. He was so on top of things and strong. He was able to do it, because he wasn't thinking of himself. But the moment he had a few minutes when there was no catastrophe to solve, he started thinking of himself, and he started suffering. He sat in his car and broke down. You never saw that when he was in action. He didn't think of himself, he didn't have time. Even thinking of the wellness of his daughter caused him to suffer, because he had made the daughter an extension of himself. So worrying is for the self, nothing else. Even if you worry for someone else it is because that person is an extension of you. All the time ... when you think of yourself you suffer. When you're not there *(the ego is not there)*, you don't think of yourself. That's what I do, I am not here, so I am ready to enjoy my life!

RABIA: I have an "I" thing. I am worried about my son. What should I do?

SHARAM: The best thing you can do is to pull yourself up. Then your beautiful energies will go to the people you're close to: me, your son, to yourself, your mom. You bring blessings to everyone by putting this "I" aside. Become a strong energy for the universe ... for your son, your close friends and everybody else.

If anybody reaches higher levels ... for example Shams, Rumi's master, wasn't fully enlightened at the time he died. He came back, and he became a great master of our time, but during Rumi's time. Shams wasn't fully enlightened, but Rumi became enlightened. Shams blessed so many people even though he wasn't totally enlightened himself. By growing, the blessings spread.

The more you grow, the more people around you benefit. Even if you grow a little bit, definitely your son and your mom will receive blessings. You don't even need to do anything with them. You're here, you grow, and they get the benefits. The more you grow, the more they benefit. Not only will they get the benefit, other people will too. If you grow to a certain point and your heart opens totally, then your father will get the benefit too. *(Rabia's father passed away when she was very young).* Your parent's parents and their parents all benefit if you become enlightened. The whole world will benefit. You can do the same as the hero of that movie. He saved millions of lives. You can save millions of lives by becoming enlightened. Just keep growing.... Every time we become aware of something, we grow slowly, but sweetly. So every time you remember there is no "I", laugh and enjoy. This week was great; I want to stretch it to one more week.

PERFECT HARMONY

SHARAM: Being in tune with someone means that you listen to them and you don't bring yourself or your ego between the two of you.

LOVE THEM ANYWAY

NIKA: You have said that when people separate themselves from others, they suffer and those around them feel guilty also. Why is that?

SHARAM: First we have to find out what the problem is. You know that when they close themselves and separate themselves from you, they suffer, and at the same time they send a subtle message out that says, "This is *your* fault. *You* have separated from *me* and I am suffering." You have to understand that there are different people on Earth with many different personalities. They are in your life so that you can understand more and learn to give them space. Before we learn to give space to others, we are easily bothered by everything.

NIKA: I see you doing that with people. Giving them space no matter how closed they are. You open yourself to them and sometimes they come around and sometimes they don't. Even then you don't get bothered. With me, when I see them closed, I close myself right away.

SHARAM: That's because I see that they have an issue, and I know that it is *their* issue. I don't need to fall into it. I do what I need to do and I leave. My ego doesn't get involved. You have to get to a point where you open yourself to them regardless of them being closed.

NIKA: Can you explain why I should do that?

SHARAM: Because you want to go higher. You should focus on yourself, not on them. If you close yourself, *you* suffer. So it is your choice. If you don't want to suffer, open yourself, don't resist, and you will be happy. Don't worry about them. They can be as closed as they want to be.

NIKA: But as soon as I open myself to them when they are closed, they want to dominate me. They treat me like I am below them.

SHARAM: This means that your homework is getting harder.

NIKA: What should I do when they want to dominate me?

SHARAM: Just pay attention that they want to do that and know that it is okay. Don't fall into it. This is doing nothing, really, it is not doing something. If you want to do something, again, you have to confront them, and get mad at them. This is not giving space. If you want to give space, don't do anything. Just look and see that this is how things are. When you can do this, you won't fall into their game; you won't feel that pressure anymore.

NIKA: Why don't we like it when they separate themselves?

SHARAM: Because we all want to become united. Unity is what we all long for and when they separate themselves, they break that unity, and everyone suffers.

Acceptance brings us to the present
and joy comes.

☙ SHARAM ❧

HELL

SHARAM: It is very interesting that we create everything around us. We make the hell around us. Our minds create everything, but higher than that is the fact that it is necessary for us. That's why we create it.

NIKA: Why is it necessary to have hell around us?

SHARAM: Because sometimes you need to clean a huge chunk of karma, so you need to fall into problems and struggle. When we suffer, old karmas come to the surface and can be released. In this way, you burn the karma. Hell means fire; it burns our karma, but it cannot burn our soul. You can never burn a soul. When someone has a lot of karma, they go to hell *(They have hellacious experiences where they suffer—emotionally, mentally, and/or physically a lot)* and in hell they burn a lot of karma. So we shouldn't be afraid of hell because nothing happens to your soul. Even if they put an atom bomb in your soul, nothing happens to it. The karma around us is like mineral calcification in water pipes that has to be removed. It is hard to get off. That hardship is hell.

LOVE IS GIVING THEM HELL

SHARAM: When people are close to each other, they are open to each other's ego. What this means is when they see the other person's ego, they hit it on the head. *(They give them hell for it.)* In fact, Existence is hitting the ego through them.

GETTING INSULTED

SHARAM: Whenever we feel insulted it means that we don't want to work on ourselves. When we feel like this, the ego comes up and either bullies the other or it feels that it has been bullied by them. Then the ego falls apart, which means we are no longer in the moment and we don't want to understand anything. It means that we are being played by our ego. So somebody makes fun of us and because the ego is our surface, you look at the situation superficially and you fall apart.

We have to learn from everything and everyone. Anytime someone makes fun of you, you have to pay attention to see why it has happened. The other day someone asked me for advice. She said that she knows a teenager and this teenager is not very happy because people make fun of her all the time. I told her that you should talk to the girl and ask her, "What is your weak point, the thing that people make fun of about you? Let's understand it and work on it." It is the same for everyone. If people make fun of you, you have to look at it and see if it truly is a weak point. If you don't have a weak point, then that making fun doesn't mean anything. It could be just a joke. But if there is a weak point, then the making fun was serious, which helps us to look at ourselves.

MAYA: It's not always making fun that bothers me. Sometimes, for example, I ask you if I should get ready, "Are we going?" and you say, "Yes." So I get ready and you say, "Oh we are not going." It bothers me that you already knew we were not going, but you told me to get ready anyway.

SHARAM: It is not like that. Something comes up and everything changes. But even if it was like that, Existence is working with you, giving you a message that you shouldn't do things for a goal or result. If you have a goal, you become a loser in life. Even if you change your clothes ten times, it does not bother you if you don't have a goal. You should enjoy what you are doing at the moment. If you are free of goals and you live in the moment, your life becomes blissful. This is what Existence is trying to tell you. When you are very serious, you get hurt and that shows that you don't want to look at your weak point. What is your weak point? Your weak point is that you are not flexible. If you don't look at things with playfulness, you can't work on yourself. Every time we get hurt, it shows that we don't want to work on ourselves. Everything that happens has a reason, even if an ant bites you or a Joe Blow insults you. Everything has a higher purpose; we just have to understand it.

MAYA: You said that if we get offended by something, that shows that we don't want to work on ourselves. But when I have very strong conditionings about something and my button is pushed, I can't do anything about it. It is not that I don't want to, I just can't.

SHARAM: When you want something with your heart, with your whole being, then it becomes easy. When you are aware, you want to work on yourself. But you are not aware all the time, so in that moment of unawareness you don't want to work on yourself.

*Really, when others critisize you,
Existence is criticizing you,
because it wants you to move,
it loves you so much,
it wants you to grow,
to drop this ego,
and be free.*

෨ SHARAM ෨

FEAR
FRESH LEMONADE FOR THE SOUL

DEBBY: I am experiencing some intense fear these days. What's happening?

SHARAM: We've been taught from childhood that when negative things come up, like fear, it's bad. So we don't like it. But we have to look at it as a very good friend, our best friend. Fear is a very positive thing. Then when it comes up, and we catch it and see it as a friend, we will feel refreshed; it refreshes us. It's like a beautiful lemonade, a glass of lemonade.

DEBBY: I'm not sure I understand that and I am wondering where this fear is coming from?

SHARAM: There are millions of stars, so many galaxies, and thousands of planets in Existence. Existence is unlimited, there is just no limit. For us, because we have a very small body and very small eyes, it all seems so big. Imagine for a small fish or a bug it's even bigger.

When the soul is free from this body and these eyes and this mind, it is as big as the unlimited—it's one with Existence. Your being is unlimited; we have the unlimited in a small thing, our body. Isn't that interesting? Everything, the whole, is included in our small body. That is the real us. There is no fear in the whole. But the way we look at life is pseudo, it's not real. We are here to go beyond our body and see the vastness of our being.

Definitely this fear is not coming from your soul. I assure you. It comes from somewhere other than the real you. It comes from many, many years of being animals and birds and then humans. The soul is fearless. It doesn't matter where it comes from, it's not you. And the only way to see that it's not you is remembering that this is a friend. A friend is not you. A friend is always somebody else. It's a friend that we have turned into an enemy. But it's really a friend. It's trying to tell you that you are beyond any fear. It's a reminder that you are not fear. That's all. The fear comes, so you remember that "I am beyond this," and when you remember, it is so refreshing. We need lots of reminders. Just that, a reminder that you are beyond fear.

A friend is a guest. Guests come any day. What's wrong with today? Today is as good a day as any other day for a friend to come and remind us. As a matter of fact, it's good for fear to come every day. Existence doesn't have any meaning. There is no why to it. It just happens. The more fear comes, the luckier you are because you have more reminders that it's not you. Any negativity that comes up is a reminder that you are not it.

Millions and millions and millions of suns. Ours is one tiny sun amongst millions of suns. This is one galaxy, but there are so many other galaxies. It's just mind boggling. The mind is so tiny and the body is so small. However, the soul is everything. All these millions of suns and galaxies are like a tiny thing for our soul. They're nothing. For us, it's big, because we look at it with the mind. We look at all these suns and we say wow, where does it stop? But for the soul, all that is nothing. Our soul is unlimited. It is sacred. How can fear be part of it? This is just a reminder that you are the soul, not the mind.

CAUTION
DO NOT WASH IN WORRY SHRINKAGE WILL OCCUR!

SHARAM: When we are afraid or worried, our soul shrinks. When the soul shrinks, we cannot become one with Existence because unity happens when we are vast, relaxed, and water-like. Imagine a piece of ice. It just stands there, but steam can move, spread, and become one with everything around it.

HIDING

NIKA: This morning you said, "People hide all the time. Some people hide behind their ego and some literally hide someplace, so they don't have to face others." I realized that I used to hide by not expressing myself all the time. Recently, I have started expressing myself more, and I feel that a layer of fear has been removed from my being. What was that fear?

SHARAM: That is the fear of others. Everyone is constantly worried about what other people think of them. By expressing yourself, you have let go of some of that fear.

NIKA: Do I express myself enough?

SHARAM: You should not approach it like this, because again you are thinking like you are at school and you want to get good grades. There is no such a thing as enough. Just do it as much as you can and don't create a goal.

WITHDRAWING

Sharam said something Chris didn't like and she is angry.

SHARAM: You either withdraw or get angry. But when you come up here and you understand something, you come to the middle. Then you are happy. But *first*, you always either withdraw or you are angry. There is no in-between unless you understand something. It brings you to the moment. All the desires go away. You really experience the moment when you have understanding.

CHRIS: Do you want me to change from what I am?

SHARAM: Apparently *you* want to change from what you are. Not me.

CHRIS: But the withdrawing makes you not look at me, so then I get angry and ruin the energy of this space.

SHARAM: No. The withdrawal comes from fear and anger. When you withdraw, you are already angry, so you push me and everyone else away. Then you get more angry because I am not looking at you, but you push people away first with the withdrawal. Withdrawal is one technique people use to get attention. Again, it all comes from fear. You have used it here a lot and you have gotten good results. Every time you withdrew you got attention.

CHRIS: So I'm always at fault.

SHARAM: Yes. Anyone who withdraws is at fault. Withdrawal is not something positive. It is something negative, and fault is always negative too. So they go together. They all come from fear. There are only two things: fear and love. There are many, many labels for fear. Withdrawal is one of the labels. Feeling bad is another. Feeling jealousy or anger, all of these are other labels. All of it is fear. And then there is love. With love, there are labels too—compassion, feeling good, laughter. They all come from love. You have a problem with laughter. When someone laughs, they love, and if you think their laughter is loud and bothers you, then love bothers you. Of course, love bothers fear, and fear bothers love. Two parts in you are bothering each other. They are fighting—a fight between fear and love. *(Talking to the group)* Chris is always in fear. That is why she says she is always at fault. Definitely she is, because she withdraws. Withdrawing is the fault, is the fear, is the negative. Again, we don't want to say fault, or wrong, or mistake. All those are different labels for one thing—fear, or negativity. So, to make your life simpler, just say "negativity, positivity" or "fear, love." That's it. It makes it *so* simple. Right now, I'm not condemning her, I'm just sharing the games of the ego. The highest thing that can happen is to accept and love your negativity. That's where you become enlightened.

DEBBY: The negativity is just the fear?

SHARAM: Yes. It is all fear. Raw fear. Raw and organic *(smiles)*.

DEBBY: When you say accept the negativity, does that mean to accept and love the fear?

SHARAM: Yes. Fear is near and is real and is good. It has been helping us immensely. We are alive because of the fear. At one point, when we are mature, we won't need fear anymore. We will understand it deeply. Then it will be gone. Then love is gone too. All that is left is beyond both. Only Existence "is." Some people might call it compassion. Some people call it divine. Some call it nothingness. Some people call it God. Don't name it. There is no name for it. The Beyond? Even that is a name. Some masters become quiet about it. Buddha became quiet, so people thought he didn't believe in God.

FEAR OF THE UNKNOWN

SHARAM: I notice that when we use one word like ego, or now we use the word fear, they really lose their meaning. What is fear? What is ego? Basically, they are fear of the unknown. The mind wants security all the time. Why do we control? We want to make sure we know what will happen next. So this unknown we are afraid of actually *is* God. We are afraid of God. We are afraid of Existence. That is again the ego.

RABIA: It feels like fear and ego are interchangeable.

SHARAM: Yes. They are the same thing, because the ego wants to say I am everything and if there is something beyond me, that is scary. Existence is beyond, and because it is the unknown, we don't know what will happen. The ego is so afraid. Fear. There is lots of fear in you. It makes you miserable. You said, "I feel so miserable." It is really the unknown that makes us miserable. We are always afraid something negative might happen.

*People first learn controlling
by controlling themselves.
Then they extend it to others
and they control others.*

∽ SHARAM ∽

LAUGH IT OUT

CHRIS: You asked me to laugh the other day. I laugh all day long at work, but here, I can't do it. I am afraid.

SHARAM: You will break a big barrier if you can laugh. It takes a while to break barriers. We keep working at it. So far, every time I remind you to laugh, you won't do it, but one day you *will*. This is how to break barriers. First we recognize the issue, the problem, then we do something about it.

CHRIS: I keep looking at it.

SHARAM: Before, looking at it was enough. Now it isn't. At some point, you have to *do* it. You just have to do it. You *can* break the fear.

CHRIS: Where is all this fear coming from?

SHARAM: The fear comes from childhood, from the family. If you laugh, you think people will not like you, they won't approve. Fear. Fear of being loud. It is very clear. With your family, if even one time they get mad at you, they won't talk to you for a long, long time. It comes from that fear of people leaving you. It is in your mind. It comes from childhood, but we want to break that barrier. We want to break that limitation. Gradually we will pass that. We just saw it very clearly right now.

CHRIS: Why is the resistance to these things so strong still? I know it comes from when I was small, but I would think that over time, working with you, that would change.

SHARAM: No, because these are memories of the past. How does a memory change? The memories never change. It is impossible. The effect that the memory has over your emotions doesn't change easily, but if you break those emotional barriers with conscious effort—for example, laughing even if you don't want to—by and by those barriers become smaller, and they won't have a hold on you anymore.

*The only way to laugh
is to forget the memories
and information of the past.
Laughing is a very subtle mechanism
that allows these memories to step aside.
When you laugh, you bring freshness.
All the memories and information step back.
You get a glimpse of the moment.
It's beautiful, so wonderful,
when I see you guys laugh.
I see that you are in touch
with that freshness.*

∽ SHARAM ∽

EXPRESS YOUR WAY TO A BEAUTIFUL LIFE

SHARAM: When you cannot express yourself, you become uncomfortable, unhappy. Your energy becomes negative. Then the people around you start thinking negative things. But when you express yourself, your energy doesn't become negative and neither does theirs, so you will have a delightful life.

Happiness means to be in this moment.

∽ SHARAM ∽

THE SECRET OF EXPRESSION

SHARAM: When we cannot express ourselves, we have to shout or yell or get angry to get things out, but if we learn how to express ourselves, we don't need any of that. When you cannot express yourself it is like being in prison. There is no freedom.

The male is strong and is able to express, but when you are more male, there really isn't much to express. Male is mechanical, it can express but the interesting and subtle things come from the female. Female has the subtlety of sensing and feeling and has a lot to say, but by herself, the female cannot express. If there is no male, it is impossible for her to express. When the female doesn't have enough male, it feels a lot of things, some positive and some negative, but because she cannot express herself, she gets frustrated. She shouts or yells. The male also gets frustrated. Because the male has his female pushed down (*he has repressed it*), he feels something but not clearly enough to express it, so he gets frustrated, but he expresses his frustration through fighting or bullying. It is destructive. Female alone without male is also destructive. Her destructiveness is not as obvious, it is more subtle. She sabotages herself or others in subtle ways because she doesn't have the tools to express herself.

So the male is the tool and the female is the depth. If they come together, we can express. There is another very interesting point here. For example, you might have both a strong male and a strong female side, but if these two are not at peace with each other then again, you cannot express. Because they don't get along, when the male is up, the female hides. It is being pushed down by the male and vice versa. When the female is there, the male is not there because female doesn't like the male. So, again, expression becomes impossible. Therefore it is very important for the male and female inside to be at peace with one another. When these two come together and are friends, life becomes fun.

PEACEMAKER

NIKA: How do I make peace with myself?

SHARAM: You have to not resist.

NIKA: Not resist what?

SHARAM: Anything. Everything that comes up that you resist.

NIKA: But how does that work?

SHARAM: You get upset and you don't express yourself. That is resistance. You are repressing your female by not expressing your emotions. If you start expressing, your female does not get repressed by your male anymore and they come to peace with each other. This means that you come to peace with yourself, and you can start understanding more subtle things. Your life will change. When we resist, it means that the conscious and unconscious are resisting each other. Basically, it means that we are resisting ourselves. The unconscious is all the things we don't like. In your case, your conscious is male and your unconscious is female, because you had a problem with your mother and you liked your father. So when you don't repress your female anymore by not resisting, your female will come out and will make friends with your male.

THE KEY TO YOUR SOUL

CHRIS: I feel like life is meaningless.

SHARAM: You spend all your life not accepting. All these exercises and meditations are necessary because you don't accept anything. If you accept, no meditations, no breathing exercises are necessary. You are in ecstasy. You breathe deeply and slowly automatically when you accept. *All* these meditations and breathing exercises are there to help you reach just a little bit of acceptance, so your breathing can touch your depth, which is total relaxation, acceptance, and love. All this so you might find a little enjoyment. Your life is meaningless because you constantly resist, because you're constantly not accepting something. Meaning comes from the depths, which is love and ecstasy. Ecstasy is the only meaning in life. You aren't in ecstasy because you are constantly fighting. You keep resisting. The only thing holding you back is that you reject everything. If you can't find anything around you to reject, you bring in some memories from the past to reject. You have to reject something all the time. We shouldn't call ourselves human beings. We should call ourselves rejecters. Human rejecters. Why are you here? You are here to do meditation and breathing. Why?

Because it will get you to a point where you let go of a little bit of your resistance, of your rejecting. It will get you to acceptance—pure acceptance—even for a moment. Then you really go into ecstasy.

When you let go during meditation, what happens? You come to acceptance. You stop resisting, you stop rejecting, for a small moment. That is what keeps you coming back to meditation, because you get to your soul; you experience your soul for a short time. When you have acceptance, you relax so much that your relaxation becomes exactly the same amount of relaxation as that of Existence. You and Existence become one. You come together, like an overlay, you coincide. There is a unity. Existence is pure joy, pure ecstasy. You will feel that. That is what your soul is. Your soul is Existence, but the mind is constantly fighting, resisting, rejecting, and conflicting.

If there is no rejecting or resisting, you are in ecstasy. I don't see you guys walking around in ecstasy. Mostly I see people disturbed, because they are fighting with themselves, with other people, with memories, with something in the future that might happen or not, with desiring. Desiring takes you away from relaxation. It is immense pressure—just simple desiring; wanting or not liking something. Love is wonderful because it brings unity. In love, you feel ecstatic because in love you accept. You accept everything totally.

*Breath is a bridge to meditation.
What does that mean?
Meditation means
our inner being coming out
and breath is a bridge.
If you can do something about your breath,
if you can breathe deeply right now
—three deep breaths—
you will come to the present.
Breath brings acceptance in,
or in other words,
with deep breath, the inner,
which is the soul,
comes to the surface.*

∽ SHARAM ∽

TENSION IN THE LINE

NIKA: You told me I resist all the time. Where does all my resistance come from?

SHARAM: It comes from parents and society. They teach you to resist all the time because, as a child, you needed to be able to protect yourself from the harshness of society and the environment. That's why you resist all the time, so you can survive in society and the world. But now you are past that point, so you don't need to resist. If you don't resist, you open yourself and the energy of Existence can come through and clean all your karma. You become blissful. You become enlightened. The only way to do this is by looking at your resistance, looking at it, not to stop it, because stopping it is impossible. In fact, trying to stop anything creates repression and you are worse off. So just look when you resist, just pay attention to it.

NIKA: But would that be enough? Just looking at my resistance doesn't seem to be enough.

SHARAM: Again, you are resisting. Just now I gave you a simple, but very strong, tool to work with, and you don't think it is enough.

NIKA: But I have done this before; it doesn't seem to work.

SHARAM: Another resistance. Yes, this didn't work for the person you were yesterday, but every day you change so much. Today, it might work. You don't even say it didn't work, you say, "It doesn't work." Again, that is resisting.

NIKA: I still feel torn apart inside.

SHARAM: Because I didn't give you the fish. I taught you how to fish. I gave you a tool. Now you have to go and practice fishing. You might not feel good right now, but you have a precious tool to work with. In fact, I gave you a fish, but a small one.

NIKA: How come you give me a small fish, but you give others big fish?

SHARAM: This is another resistance, but it also has a great lesson in it. I do that because everyone is different. I give people fish until they get to a point where they can catch a fish themselves. This is wonderful: not only did we catch resistance, but we caught a lesson along with it. These are keepers!

The next day....

NIKA: What I realized from yesterday, is that every time I don't like something or I find something hurtful, instead of looking at it or going into it, I want to escape from it by ignoring it or changing the subject. So I repress it, and then I can't see it to open it and talk about it.

SHARAM: Not expressing is resisting." You don't look at things, you don't express them, so you resist. This happens all the time. All these small resistances pile up and make a big mountain of resistance. Your only way out of this is to pay attention every time you resist. Go into the hurt and express it.

NIKA: Is going into it and expressing it a big chunk of the answer to my problem?

SHARAM: It's not a chunk of it; it's almost all of it. The rest is easy; it comes with understanding.

LIKE A WEED

SHARAM: If somebody says to me, "But this is different from what you said before," that shows that they have not understood deeply what I told them just now. If they understood it, they would never even think of what has been said before. They would know that Existence grows all the time. How can it say the same thing to you today as it said yesterday? You have grown since yesterday. You are a different person.

GOD
THE EMPTY SPACE BETWEEN YOUR EARS

Sharam is talking to one of the students about being sleepy in class:

SHARAM: When we resist, we lose energy, but if we don't resist, the energy of Existence will pour into us. Existence will help us to get through everything and anything. Like right now we talked about you being sleepy in class, and for first time you didn't resist. You got a little upset, but mostly you wanted to go into it and find out what is going on. This is what I call not resisting. When we do this, Existence comes in and takes care of the problem. So let's go into it and see why you get sleepy in class. One of the reasons is resistance. Resistance means bringing the mind in, starting to think about what was said, rationalizing it, having inner talk about it, or opposing it. But listening without resistance, from the heart, means that you listen but you don't think about it. Just being with the subject, totally, without inner talk and bargaining is what I call not resisting. So one new meaning of resistance is bringing the mind in because the mind is always bargaining and going against everything. It doesn't trust, it wants to find a problem, or something wrong with what it hears. It wants to twist it to serve its own purposes.

*The energy of Existence is plentiful
and available to everyone.
We receive this energy
according to our own capacity and quality.
If we have higher quality,
we receive more,
we sense more.*

∽ SHARAM ∽

OLD PATTERNS

*If, in this very moment,
you can breathe deeply
you will come to the now.*

◈ SHARAM ◈

DEBBY: I am in debt again and I'm paying a large amount in interest to the credit card companies each month. I've done this many times before.

SHARAM: If we are in debt, we create that. If we pay this debt off, then we create another debt. It's good to have money that we owe to the bank; otherwise we just go and borrow more. That owing money to the bank is holding you back from going and borrowing more. So it's worth it to pay a lot of money in interest, so we don't borrow more. But definitely, we have created it. This is your pattern.

DEBBY: So, if we become aware of our patterns, will they change?

SHARAM: Actually we can look even deeper. Why does this happen? How does awareness change the outside? Awareness brings relaxation. Relaxation will change the breathing. The breathing will go deeper and slower. When the breathing goes deeper and slower, you will feel more connected with the original self, which is love, and all fears will go away. When there is no fear, you have a fresh look every moment. You have a fresh look at the situation, a look with no fear and this will create a new you. You will be different from there on. Things will change. Patterns will break. You won't be stuck anymore. Acceptance does a lot for you. The only reason the pattern persists, the reason we are stuck, is because we are not relaxed. We have fear. Acceptance changes all that.

What just happened is magic!

BABA: And then when we are changed, people mirror us; they are no longer hard on us, the outside changes according to our inside.

SHARAM: Yes Baba, that is great. What Baba said was very interesting. When there is no fear, other people will reflect you. They become a mirror.

BABA: No fear makes us relaxed and since other people mirror us they become relaxed towards us. Then they are not hard on us.

SHARAM: Very good. It's all our reflection. Everything. Every single thing outside, basically, has something to do with our inside.

Also, let's say you feel pain somewhere in your body, a tiny pain, and your mind goes to the worst case scenario. Maybe it says, "I knew it! I have cancer!" What happens here? You are afraid. You shrink. When your soul shrinks with fear, fresh juice, the fresh energy of Existence cannot go into you. That fresh energy can heal anything. But you are afraid. You are squeezing your soul. There is no room for fresh energy to come in. Without that energy, you will create that illness you fear, or worse even, because you don't get fresh energy to heal yourself. But when you accept, when you say Existence knows better and there is nothing to worry about, fear goes away. And the shrinking of the soul, this compression of the soul, doesn't happen. The soul opens up. It's not fearful. And then new energy pours in and whatever problem is in the body will be solved. You will be healed. Fear doesn't let you get healed.

OLD COUPLES

NIKA: When people have been together for long time, mostly they become bitter and harsh to each other. Why?

SHARAM: Because the unconscious has taken over their relationship and the unconscious is all the negativities that we don't want.

NIKA: So does that mean that they don't love each other anymore?

SHARAM: This kind of love, love between a man and women has degrees, because, when you love that person, you also hate them deep inside. If the love is up right now, the hate is buried underneath; and if the hate is up, know well that the love is underneath. This goes for everything. If you love something, you hate it at the same time; the two poles are always together. But if you care deeply about something and don't love it or hate it, we call that the middle path, which will take us to the beyond. This is the higher love. It is above duality.

WISDOM OF HATE

MELINA: You mentioned that if we love someone, we hate them too. How can I go beyond that?

SHARAM: You should not be afraid of hate. Hate has its own wisdom. If you understand the subtleties of it, what's behind it, you will know the wisdom of hate. If you don't have understanding, then hate is bad and we have to be afraid of it. As long as you can bring understanding into things, you should not be afraid. It is like a virus that is very dangerous. If we don't know what it is, it can kill us, but if we learn about it, we can find the cure for it and there is nothing to be afraid of. If you feel hate towards me it is easy. Whatever comes up, we talk about it and the subtleties of the issue open up. However, with others, because their ego might get involved, it is harder. When the ego is up, they defend themselves and it is harder to work through it. But even then, you can talk to me about it and we bring the understanding in together.

BEING SPECIAL

KATE: Could you talk about wanting to be special please?

SHARAM: Being special means separating yourself from Existence, which is not real, because you cannot separate yourself from Existence. It is an illusion. That's why, when you feel special, you get hurt, because you go to illusion. Whenever we go to illusion and separate ourselves from Existence, we become miserable. The misery comes to take us back to Existence again. Like right now all my attention is on you for a while, we call that being special or getting energy from Existence. We want this attention all the time. When you want it to be there all the time, that's what wanting to be special is. You don't want the attention to go somewhere else. Attention is like food. You eat until you get full, then you don't eat anymore. If you eat food all the time, you get sick. Same with attention; you get some and when you don't need it anymore, the attention goes somewhere else. If it stays on you too long (like movie stars or rock stars), you won't want it anymore, you'll get frustrated. You will start rejecting it. Then you start hating attention. You can't receive love anymore. Existence always gives us the right amount of attention. If the attention is more than we need, we suffer. Because, even that thing that we wanted so much doesn't have any attraction for us anymore. Everything loses its meaning in life. One wants to commit suicide. So, Existence regulates the amount of attention for us. We just have to trust Existence. Existence knows what's best for us.

THE SOUNDS OF EGO

MAYA: Sharam and I went for a walk by the river for my sitting. As soon as we started walking, Sharam started collecting rocks. We only talked about one issue for a few minutes, and very soon he had so many rocks, we had to come back. I got bothered and said, "Sharam, it seems like you don't care about me and my sitting. Is that right?"

SHARAM: In general, there is no such thing as "Nobody cares about me or they don't pay attention to me." We always get as much attention as we need, but the ego always wants to get more. That's why it says, "He doesn't pay attention to me at all." The reason we left the river wasn't that I don't care. There are a thousand and one reasons why we left. Maybe it was dangerous, maybe because it was cold outside, we might have caught a cold. We were only there to understand one thing and we did our job. We talked about one thing; we learned what we needed to learn about that one thing and we left. When we learned that one thing, we were done. That space gave us what it was supposed to give us. The rest was a waste of time, so Existence took us out of there immediately.

The ego always thinks of itself, it always wants more, it always thinks that others are putting it down. The ego wants extreme respect, but no matter how much you give to it, it doesn't get satisfied. It wants more. So it is very interesting that the ego goes right away to "They are mean to me, they want to put me down; I better defend myself, or repress or get upset." All of this is because of an ego that is never satisfied. But remember everything that happens has a thousand and one reasons that we don't understand, and thinking that they did this because they don't care about me is just the sound of ego.

I WANT TO LIKE MYSELF

MAYA: Why don't I like myself?

SHARAM: The more they have told us, "You are not good enough, you are not doing a good job, you should be better," the less we like ourselves. In one way or another they tell us, "You are wrong, you don't know anything, you are good for nothing." That's why we don't like ourselves. The more space they gave us, the more we like ourselves. If they never said negative things about us and they stayed very positive and supportive with us, then we can like ourselves. It is very simple. If you are liked by your parents, you can like yourself.

MAYA: If our parents were not like what you described, and we are adults now, what do we do?

SHARAM: You have to grow your consciousness so that whenever you see that you don't like yourself—you are condemning yourself, putting yourself down, regretting what you have done—you remember that Existence wanted all this, and if Existence wants something, there is nothing wrong with it. The more we trust Existence, the more we trust and like ourselves. Your trust has grown a lot, Maya. You like yourself much more. Your life has changed a lot. When you like yourself, you don't condemn others either. If your liking becomes one hundred percent, we call that love. Love is from the Beyond. It is very different than liking.

CRITICISM IS HARD TO ACCEPT

SHARAM: Because we don't have acceptance for ourselves, we cannot accept other people's criticism.

LIKING YOURSELF AND OTHERS

MAYA: Why don't we like someone?

SHARAM: The amount that we like ourselves is the amount that we like others. The main question is, what does it mean to like yourself and how can you like yourself more? The more we trust Existence, the more we like ourselves. When we trust, the negative feelings are not there. When we have negativity inside, we don't like ourselves and we don't trust Existence. Trusting means there is no jealousy, because when you trust, you don't ask why somebody has more than you do. The same is true with anger. We get angry because we don't like something or we feel insulted, but if we trust that everything is perfect, is necessary, then we are happy. The more we get angry, then, the less we trust Existence and the less we like ourselves. So the more we trust, the more positive we become, and the more we like ourselves and others.

If we don't like someone; if we think others are this and that, we are fooling ourselves. No one else exists. We always like to say others are at fault. We say they don't have love and so on and so forth. This only shows that we don't want to understand something deeper. If we want to understand the depths of the problem, we should know that no one else exists. This is the way an adult looks at the world. Whatever happens, I am creating it.

MAYA: What does trusting Existence have to do with liking myself?

SHARAM: When you trust Existence, you become calm, centered. When you are calm and centered, then you can like yourself and others. In old times, people liked each other more. Today everything is so fast, nobody is centered. Everybody is in a rush.

MAYA: The fact that they told us we are not good enough, how does that fit in here?

SHARAM: We are in a rush because we want to make ourselves seem better. We want to make more money so people will like us more. If they hadn't told you that you weren't good enough, you would have stayed calm and centered; you wouldn't need to rush. You would trust Existence and like yourself and others.

MAYA: Is it possible that one day a miracle will happen and I will all of a sudden trust Existence, or do I have to do it myself?

SHARAM: That *is* what we call miracle!

MAYA: *(laughter)* How is that a miracle if I have to do it myself?

SHARAM: You are Existence, aren't you? So if Existence is doing it, it is a miracle.

MAYA: So in every situation where I find myself not liking myself or another, I have to see that I have not trusted and change that. Is that right?

SHARAM: You don't need to change it. Every time you see that you aren't trusting, at that moment you are trusting. You are aware that you are not trusting. Awareness is trust. Awareness is everything. Awareness means deep understanding. Awareness means seeing, witnessing. This is where everything comes together—love, trust, awareness, understanding, etc. You just need to be aware and pay attention.

THE BENEFITS OF NOT LIKING YOURSELF

SHARAM: It doesn't matter what the problem is; the only thing that matters is to be able to witness. You could be a beggar like Buddha, but when you have witnessing, you have everything. The problems we have, we don't like, because when we don't like something, we pay attention to it. That's the whole point. It helps to make our witnessing strong. You can be anybody— a beggar, a president, a cook—and witness. Many enlightened people were tailors or porters or they didn't even have a job, but they became enlightened because they were witnessing. So if you feel you are a failure and you don't like it, it's very good because something you don't like, you pay attention to. Because society disapproves of it, you worry about it. Anything that you think is bad you want to change, so your witnessing becomes strong. That's the only thing that matters. Nothing else matters. All problems are there so we can distance ourselves from them, so we can witness.

NIKA: I don't accept my problems. I don't like them.

SHARAM: If you liked them you couldn't work on them. The reason you can work is that you don't like them. If you liked everything, your witnessing could not become strong. Existence has planned it so that at first there are many things you don't like about yourself. Then you will want to work on yourself. When the witnessing becomes strong, then all of a sudden, you like everything. Of course the best is to like everything, but we are not there yet. So the best for us right now is to not like these things. Then we can witness and when we do, we will get where we like everything. We come to a deep let-go.

NIKA: So when they say, "Love yourself," it really doesn't mean anything. Because you are not supposed to like your problems, you just have to witness them; and when you become a witness, then you like everything anyway.

SHARAM: When they say "Love yourself," it means that you should have acceptance for yourself. But when you can't do that, the deeper acceptance is to accept that you cannot accept and know that it is okay that you don't like your problems, and that there is a benefit even in that. So you see whatever is, is okay. It is the way it should be. Everything is perfect.

WHAT COLOR'S YOUR CARPET?

RABIA: I feel bad. I hear from everyone how hurtful I can be, but I don't listen. I don't do what I need to, to grow. Can you help me?

SHARAM: You're right ... you're not.... Okay, let's look at this. This area over here *(pointing to a red carpet on the floor)* is where people who don't grow hang out. They just want to feel bad, and get mad at themselves and others. As long as you are here *(on the red carpet)* you can't be over there *(pointing to a blue carpet on the other side of the room)*. The blue carpet is where growth, happiness and love is. You keep saying, "I feel bad," and you continue to stand here on this red carpet. As long as you choose to stay on that carpet, my hands are tied.

RABIA: Okay. I don't want to be on this carpet anymore.

SHARAM: Then move.

RABIA: How?

SHARAM: Just don't feel bad and you will no longer be standing on that red carpet. It's a catch twenty-two. You are standing there saying, "I hate being here; I don't like it. I feel bad," so your focus remains on the negative, on the red carpet. You keep promoting being on the red carpet. So you are promoting being there by being there. As long as you feel bad, sad, mad, or angry, you're standing on the red carpet, and nobody can do anything for you.

RABIA: So how do I get out of here?

SHARAM: Acceptance is how you get out of there. Giving space to yourself is how you get off the red carpet. You're not doing that. You are standing on this red carpet, not accepting anything. You're mad and sad, thinking, "This is horrible. I don't like this. I hate it." So you just keep reinforcing staying right where you are. But when you accept, all of a sudden you're not there; you're here on this blue carpet. It's all in your hands. I can't do anything.

Me, I'm over here on this blue carpet. I keep accepting everything in my life. I'm inviting you to come and join me, but you insist on being sad and mad. What can I do?

Accept and you'll be on the blue carpet. Give space to yourself and others and you'll be on the blue carpet. Understand, and you'll be on the blue carpet. It's simple: Blue carpet, real happiness, ecstasy, things work out for the best, and miracles happen. Red carpet: Misery, misery, and more misery. Nothing but misery.

You have to accept that everything that is happening is perfect.

RABIA: How do I accept that everything I am is okay? Everyone else has so many problems with me, with how I am.

SHARAM: If you are crying, accept it. If you are unhappy, accept it. Just tell yourself it's fine.

RABIA: How can it be fine? It's not fine with you. It's not fine for the people I live with. So how can it be fine for me?

SHARAM: If it is fine for you, it will be fine for everyone else—if it is not fine with others it just shows that you are standing there willingly on the red carpet thinking, "This is terrible, I am terrible." It is only when we reject something about ourselves that others reject that thing in us. If we don't like it, they don't like it either.

There is nobody else. There is only us. It all starts with or stems from us first. When you accept yourself, others will accept you. If you accept Melina, for example, she will accept you. If you accept a situation, give space to it, and say, "Existence wants this," then, you are free. You relax and let go. It's that simple. Anything that happens, just say, "It's perfect."

RABIA: I can say it, but really I don't feel it.

SHARAM: Because you just don't want to budge. You walk around and think you are the boss of Existence. You think, "Existence wants this? Phooey!" You keep thinking, "If God wants what is happening, he must be really crazy. There's nothing wrong with me, it's Existence making the mistake here." Every time you think, "Why is this happening, or I don't like this," you are declaring God crazy.

How do we get off the red carpet? By liking everything that has happened in the past; liking everything that will happen in the future; by *liking* everything, because Existence *is* doing it. Like Existence and Existence will like you. When you like God, you join with God, and all of a sudden you are vast. You have space and space means ecstasy. It means joy. Join Existence and you won't lose anything. You only win. There is nothing to be done. Existence wants something to happen and it's perfect, no matter what it is. God is running the show. There is no you.

RABIA: I feel put down when you say I act like the boss of Existence.

SHARAM: It is a put down because you *are* down. Everything feels like a put down because you are standing on the red carpet. Nobody can like you when you stand there. *(Sharam starts singing "Don't Stand So Close to Me," over and over again while snapping his fingers.)* That red carpet is telling everyone, "Don't stand so close to me."

PATIENCE
THE PATH TO KINDNESS

FARIN: I feel like I am an unkind person.

SHARAM: An unkind person is a person who doesn't have awareness or insight. Insight means understanding. A person who cannot or does not understand is an unkind person. On the other hand, a person could be too kind, which comes from ignorance too, from unawareness. This kind of kindness suffocates others. With too much kindness you torture people. For example, your friend is not hungry, but you insist that he should eat this delicious food. This insisting comes from your kindness, but you don't understand that he is not hungry. This kindness becomes like a torture. People start to wish that you *were* an unkind person, that you would let them breathe.

So whatever your conditioning is, you act from that. But when you gain understanding and become more aware, you will become a truly kind and also a very real person. Because the depth of everything is love, as you go deeper, you become truly kind. You will have lots of love toward everything and everyone. Then with that awareness and with that kindness, you will have ecstasy. You will enjoy yourself. Every moment of life will be full of fun and joy.

FARIN: Why is it like that? Why have I lost my kindness here in the West? I don't have patience. I don't have time for others. I feel so selfish.

SHARAM: When there is a rush, there is no room for humanity. These days, when people are talking or interacting, they are in a rush. Why? Because nobody has patience or time to spend listening to others. You need to be quick and efficient; otherwise people will get bored. Nobody has patience. Everything is about speed. Even the movies have become speedy. You can see speed in just about everything. The reason that everything has become so fast, is because of fear, fear of rejection. It comes from the ego. In order to avoid the ego getting hurt or rejected, speed has been created. If you talk to someone longer, there is possibility that you'll get rejected. In the West, we love speed only so we won't get rejected. In old times people would sit and talk and take their time to chit chat. In speed there is no humanity. Humanity needs patience, needs us to go deeper. In speed we cannot be human.

TICK-TOCK

Mind is tense because mind is not total.

DEBBY: I always feel just a little guilty when I'm late.

BABA: I always feel moderately guilty when I'm late.

ADELE: I never feel guilty because I'm always on time.

SHARAM: About meeting the criteria of our conditioning; this is very interesting. Just now, I was on the phone with a student of mine, telling him that the main thing in life for Adele is being on time, and for him it is studying. I told him if you don't do your studying, then whatever else you do, you can't be total in it, because in the back of your mind you feel guilty that you didn't do your studying. You can't really enjoy whatever it is. Then to enjoy it, you have to drink alcohol. When you get drunk, you shut down the guilt for a short while, so you can enjoy these other things you do. But more and more and more, that main thing that you are supposed to do (*studying*) doesn't get done. It doesn't get done, and more and more, you have to drink alcohol, so you can be a little bit total in whatever else you do. It comes to a point that you become addicted to alcohol, but it happens very gradually.

But if you do what you are supposed to do, if you do your studying, you feel so happy. You don't feel guilty anymore, so whatever else you do, you have fun. You don't need alcohol to have let-go. So alcohol or drugs are mostly for that reason. You feel that you are not doing what you've been conditioned to do, so you have to use drugs or alcohol to let go of that guilt.

The student said, "My conditioning is not about studying, it's about doing my spiritual work. Because I'm not doing that, I feel guilty." I told him spiritual work is not about doing meditation; there is no homework. Spiritual work is just about getting to know yourself and understanding subtle things. Earlier, in his sitting, we understood some things about him and he really enjoyed it. He had so much fun. I asked him, "Do you remember a minute ago you said that was fantastic because you understood something? Do you remember how fun it was?" He said, "It's the funnest thing in the whole world." I told him, mysticism is not about sitting there and saying Ommmmmm…. It's about understanding things, which is very exciting and fun. The best thing in the whole world is to understand. Nothing comes close to it. It is so exciting. That is mysticism. So when you try to understand yourself, when you look at yourself and you share with me, when you work on yourself, that is mysticism. Nothing else.

And remember, anytime you get anywhere is the right time with God. *(Lots of laughter)*

THE FOUNTAIN OF LIFE

CHRIS: *(Crying)* You said I need to cry more, but you also said I shouldn't fall apart?

SHARAM: Crying is not falling apart. To me, crying is a constructive thing. Falling apart means to have a fight with someone or a temper tantrum or something like that. You know what just happened here. You had this vision of the past, a memory. They told you that if you are crying, you are falling apart. This comes from society. From my angle, crying is a constructive thing. It is not falling apart. It is actually a coming together. It is the opposite of falling apart. We assume what society teaches us is true, when in reality it is 180 degrees from the truth.

The mind's interpretation of things is always different from the truth.

∞ SHARAM ∞

MESSAGES FROM THE PAST

MELINA: Sometimes a memory from the past comes up and it brings up emotions in me. Sometimes they are hurtful and sometimes not.

SHARAM: If memories come up, it is because they want to get a higher understanding and leave you forever. So if they are hurtful, it is very good because then you have to bring a new and higher understanding of them. When you have total understanding, they won't bother you anymore. You'll understand why they happened and how fortunate you were that they happened. They have a great message. Existence tries to give us a message over and over, for years and years, and finally when we don't get it, Existence says, "I better give them a big hurt, so they might get it." It tries everything it can think of for us to get it and, sometimes even with a wake-up call, we still don't get it. It usually happens later on in life, if we are lucky enough to find a path of self-discovery. Today, your understanding is that all these hurts are trying to give you a message, a lesson, that you needed to get, but you resisted because you did not have the understanding. Right now, you are ready to understand. Just bring up whatever hurt from the past that arises, and we'll talk about it, we'll go deep into it, and the message will come out easily.

WHERE IS THE LOVE?

MAYA: Sometimes people know if they do something, it will bother me, but they do it anyway. Where is the love in that?

SHARAM: When Existence doesn't cooperate with you, it is because Existence wants to work with you. It pushes you until you get it *(the lesson or understanding)*. If it didn't push you so much right now, you would have no motivation to want to understand anything. All the pressures, the problems, in life are just so that someday you'll say, "To hell with it, I want to understand this."

MAYA: So if I am more subtle, I won't need to be pushed so much? I'll get the hint the first time?

SHARAM: Exactly. Pressure is a gift to help you want to grow. You either die or understand something *(grow)*. If you die, don't worry, you'll get an even better chance to understand next time.

EVERYBODY IS HIGH

SHARAM: If somebody puts you down and wants to prove that you are nothing, that you are below them, if you get hurt, you have fallen into their game. If you just see how low they are because they put you down, that is not true either. If you think they are low and they think you are low, then you both are on the same level here. But neither of you is really low. Everybody is Existence, everybody is one, and everybody is at the same level. Everyone is really high. The fact is that the person who insulted you has a wound and if you get hurt by what they say, you have the same wound. So basically they are sending us a message: they are saying, "Don't fall into my game. Don't think that I am bad even though I am doing something negative." We should see the good in the bad and get the message that says, "Don't give in to your ego, don't get upset. Allow the understanding to come in." That is why Existence has sent them to you. That is beautiful.

DON'T GIVE IN TO THE EGO

SHARAM: The ego doesn't want us to have deeper understanding, because understanding destroys the ego. One of the tactics of the ego to avoid understanding is to make us defensive and upset. It takes us to the emotional body and we think nobody loves us. This makes it very difficult to be willing to look at ourselves and what is happening. But don't give in to the ego. Always go with understanding. Always stay open to understanding.

THE SCHOOL OF LIFE

MELINA: Why don't I like it when I get into a fight or conflict with others?

SHARAM: Because the ego doesn't like it. The ego says, "Look, they don't see how wonderful I am." The ego gets hurt. When there is a fight, it shows that Existence knows that you are ready for some homework. It's no different from homework a teacher gives a student to help them become better. On the path, there is no book homework; your homework is when someone steps on your toes and you get to see how you can handle it. Existence would not give an assignment to us if we were not ready for it.

MELINA: But the last time someone stepped on my toes, they threatened me also.

SHARAM: Well that's what fight means. Right? *(Smiles)* I don't think you get hugs and kisses in a fight.

MELINA: *(laughing)* That's true, but what do I do when I start thinking about it or remembering it, and wondering if it will happen again?

SHARAM: You bring understanding, a new look. You learn the lesson and then you thank Existence for giving you this opportunity to grow. You say to yourself, "This was homework for me, so I will become strong, and the next time something like this happens, I won't get upset." Next time, if someone attacks you, you just ask them what they are trying to say, and if it makes sense, you listen to them. Put your ego aside—maybe they are right.

However, this is only one way of looking at things. You don't have to do it. I am just saying there is a possibility to look at things without the ego. Just know that Existence is giving you homework, so you can become enlightened. How else do you want to grow? Whatever bothers you, you just need to bring a new understanding to it. If what I say makes you happy, very good; if not, that's okay also.

MELINA: It does make me happy. Thank you.

SHARAM: I'm glad. When all of a sudden we become calm and happy inside, it shows that understanding has happened.

UNDERSTANDING
THE BRIDGE BETWEEN FAITH AND AWARENESS

NIKA: Sometimes people do things that I think are wrong, but you approve of them and I don't like it.

SHARAM: If you trust Existence, you will understand that there may be a higher reason for what I do and that I am working with that person. If you get upset it means that you resisting Existence in a subtle way. Nothing is wrong in Existence. If we get upset, it shows that we don't understand. Every time you don't understand something, you resist. You don't have faith. There are two paths in mysticism: the path of awareness and the path of love. Understanding brings awareness. Love brings faith. But there is a magic with understanding. The magic is that understanding brings faith also. When we understand something we move to faith. Your path is not love. In this century, the mind has taken over our lives so much that there is no room for love and faith. We have to go through understanding to get to faith, to love. So understanding is a bridge between the Path of Love and the Path of Awareness, and both paths end in faith.

BE AWARE
AWARENESS IS COMING

CHRIS: I still get just as upset at stupid stuff. I shouldn't get upset at this stuff, because I am meditating more.

SHARAM: You have become more aware. The same stuff was happening before, but you never noticed it.

CHRIS: But with awareness comes acceptance, and there is no acceptance in me at all. None.

SHARAM: With awareness, first comes watching, and then when there is enough awareness, it turns into acceptance. Right now you just watch the negativities, and because you see them more, you hate them more. You just need the awareness to get to a certain point and all of a sudden, acceptance will come. In your sittings, we speed up the process. Together we bring understanding so awareness comes. That awareness brings acceptance and you are happy. It is not the understanding that brings acceptance. The understanding brings awareness. But because the awareness is caused by sitting with me and not by your inner awareness, again you will fall.

You see, there are two things you do here. One, you do your exercises. The other is that you have a sitting with me, like this. In the sitting, or when I share something, you get more understanding and that understanding brings some awareness and then acceptance. But because the understanding comes from the outside, from me sharing it with you, it gets lost. The understanding gets lost, because if it stays in the mind, it becomes dead and is no good. Any understanding the next day is no good. It is only good for that moment. That's why I always say, "Anything I say is only good for this moment; the next moment is totally new, with a completely different set of truths." Why have understanding then? Because it gives you awareness and that awareness stays with you.

The awareness that you gained does not get lost. Gradually you are becoming more aware, with your meditations, with your exercises, breathing exercises, me sharing things with you, and with your sittings. Up to now, those awarenesses have added up and brought you more unhappiness. Why? Because now you can see all the negativities more. They make you unhappy. All you need is a little bit more, maybe more than a little bit, of awareness *(laughter)*. The awareness piles up until, eventually, you can reach to awareness yourself (inner awareness). Inner awareness will take you to acceptance and happiness. Meanwhile we are doing it together with deeper and deeper understanding.

THE DEEPER THE ISSUE, THE LONGER IT TAKES —SOMETIMES

CHRIS: I can't get past the habit of wanting to get attention.

SHARAM: You just broke that habit by coming to talk to me. Today, you broke a habit. You came up without me having to call you.

CHRIS: Yes, but I did it aggressively.

SHARAM: Yes, it was abrupt, because you were breaking a habit, which is fine. I saw that and I was happy. I don't call that wanting attention. I call that connection. If you go with your habit, that means wanting attention. If you break it, we call that connection.

CHRIS: I condemn wanting attention. I see how much I condemn myself and others.

SHARAM: Everyone has a different issue or even if they have the same issue, they work on it differently. Yours is wanting attention.

You started with this issue when you were seven or eight years old, now fifty years have passed. Working on this with you is taking time, so we see this issue is deep. The deeper it is, the longer it takes. Of course, we keep breaking ground to get to the root of it, the depth, but still, we have to go deeper; then it will be resolved. Do you see that? If you had developed this issue when you were twenty, you would pass by it faster. If you developed this when you were thirty, faster still. But for you it was younger. So we have to go deeper and deeper until we get to the point where you pass it. Then it becomes in the domain of the known, *the conscious*. It is resolved. So we keep digging, keep digging. We are hoping to get there soon, so don't be discouraged that you still have that issue. I'm really rushing to get us there.

H-ANGRY

MONA: When I get hungry, I get very angry sometimes. Why is that?

SHARAM: When you are hungry, it means that there is not enough energy available to you. To be aware and conscious, we need energy. Therefore, if there is not enough energy, we become unaware. This means the unconscious will come up and whatever is in there starts surfacing. If you get angry it means that you have some problems inside, you don't like certain things and you have unhappiness in there. It is very interesting.

Also, it depends on whether, in that moment, if you are more male or more female. We naturally cycle from being more male to more female every forty-five minutes or so. You can tell if you are more male or female by which nostril is the most open, which one is easier to breathe through. Every forty-five minutes one of our nostrils opens up a little more and the other one closes a little bit. If the right one opens up, we become more male, and if the left one opens up, we become more female. If the right one is open, you get angry because you are male. However, if the left one is open, because it's female, you become weak and you start nagging. So it all depends on which nostril is more open at the time that you are hungry.

MOODS OF THE MOON

RANDY: Why do we have different moods all the time? Like sometimes we resist, and sometimes we don't. Does it relate to the cycles of the moon?

SHARAM: There are lots of reasons for resistance and our moods, but yes, the moon has a lot to do with our energies. Resistance is related to the moon. During the new moon we don't have much energy. When our energy level is low, we are in turmoil, and when this happens, we feel sad and down and disappointed. We don't feel angry so much during the new moon; we feel more passive. We feel hurt and keep things to our self. When we move toward a full moon, we have more energy. This high energy could turn into anger or fight. Also, low energy levels cause different illnesses than high energy levels. For example, high energy causes high blood pressure. Low energy can cause blood pressure that is too low, which will create different problems for the body. So high levels and low levels of energy lead us to resistance, and one of the causes of this imbalance is the moon. But if we are aware we just feel these highs and lows, but we don't fall into them. With awareness all the resistance subsides.

Resistance means being in the mind or thinking. The mind is about duality, so when we are in the mind, the two opposite poles (positive and negative) fight with each other all the time. Any clash of negative and positive, male and female or any opposite poles, we call resistance. When energy is not balanced, there will be fight inside or outside. When energy is not in order, we won't have inner order either. Lack of inner order we call resistance. When the energy is balanced, it drops from the mind to the soul or the body.

KUNDALINI AND DEATH

We were discussing the taboos of sex and death and how anything that brings kundalini up is feared by society.

NIKA: What does kundalini have to do with death?

SHARAM: When kundalini rises up and leaves your body, your soul goes with it. That's death.

NIKA: So when we die the kundalini awakens and it helps the soul to leave?

SHARAM: Yes.

NIKA: And then the soul doesn't have the kundalini anymore?

SHARAM: No, it does. That's why when you come back *(are born again)*, you are like an enlightened person, but you are unaware. Life allows us to awaken our kundalili at the time of death; that's why beautiful things happen in death—you see light and everything. Death is just like enlightenment, but then, when you come back, because the kundalini was not fully awakened, it closes again. So when you are born, you are enlightened but unaware. You are born again to become aware. When you are aware, totally aware, you are free to do whatever you like to do, come back as a baby or not.

The soul is not limited to time or space. The soul is everywhere all the time. You are like a piece of a puzzle. When you are alive and not enlightened, that piece of the puzzle is missing from the whole picture. But when you die or you become enlightened, the piece goes back to the puzzle. It makes it complete. You are everywhere and you feel everything. Actually the whole Existence becomes so small all of a sudden. Right now it seems so big because we are separated, we are out of it. Enlightenment or death means to go back to the all, but death is temporary. When you are born again, you get separated from the whole again.

So death is a temporary unity with Existence and it is beautiful. You have so much fun when you are not alive. But when you are born again, you bring all your conditionings from past lifetimes with you. The ego is the culmination of many past lifetimes' experiences and you bring all of these experiences with you into this lifetime. You do this because you need to continue your journey to awareness from where you left off in your last life. So everything comes with you and gradually you lose that fun and lightness of death. When you are born, for a few years you are free, but then the ego starts building up. All those conditionings come back again, and you start manipulating and dominating.

WHY LAY OVER WHEN YOU CAN GO DIRECT?

NIKA: Sometimes I say something or suggest something and you say it is wrong. But if someone else suggests the same thing, but they sugar coat it instead of being direct, you say, "Wow, how wonderful!" What should I do? Should I do what they do?

SHARAM: Now why would you want to do what they do?

NIKA: Because you tell them how high they are when they do that.

SHARAM: Yes, what they do is very high for them, but it would be very low for you.

NIKA: How is that?

SHARAM: Let me give you an example. It is like you both want to go from point A to point B, but you take different routes. Their route is up a hill and to get up the hill, they have to build steps. So when they make the steps, I say, "Wow, how wonderful!" However you are taking a route that doesn't need steps. You are going straight to point B. Why would you want to build steps? Your route doesn't even need steps. You are going straight to point B. Yet you insist, "Well, I want to make steps because you praised them when they made steps!" You have to understand that people's paths are different.

NIKA: But you said I was wrong and they were right. So I thought I should do what they do.

SHARAM: I said you were wrong because you *were* wrong. Also, I said they were right because they *were* right. Here you have to bring some deeper understanding and subtlety. You have to see that what you are doing is wrong for you, but it doesn't mean that you have to do what they do. You have to become more subtle to see that you need to transform, but you need to transform in a way that is good for you. You have to be authentic and learn to bring subtlety in your authenticity.

NIKA: *(With laughter)* Oh, I get to do all the hard work!

SHARAM: In fact, your work is much easier, because you are going straight *(taking the direct route)*. Their work is more complicated, so it takes longer for them to get there. You see, you just have to look deeper. There is another aspect to this. Your path is understanding, so I always tell you if there is something wrong. But maybe their path is love. Then I don't focus on understanding with them. I just give them love. So you see, when we look deeper, everything is in order. Existence is incredible.

RESPECT & POWER
NOT ALL THEY'RE CRACKED UP TO BE

NIKA: It feels like with me you always do and say whatever comes to you. You don't tip toe around me, but with some other people, I see you are very considerate.

SHARAM: It is good that I am this way with you. The person I am considerate with is not ready, so I cannot work with them. They have a long ways to go. If I am not considerate with you, it shows that you are more advanced.

NIKA: I feel like maybe I have something inside where I don't create respect or maybe it's not even respect; I am not sure how to express myself.

SHARAM: Respect is there because people don't have understanding. When they get into conflict, they cannot resolve it. Therefore, they better be respectful to each other so more problems are not created. They don't have the tools to work on things, so they repress and respect all the time. The harsher the society, the more respect is needed. Respect keeps people from hurting each other. In a society that has more subtle understanding, there is not much respect. So respect shows that people are distant from each other and they don't have understanding. When there is no respect, there are two possibilities. One shows that one person is stronger than the other, and he bullies the other person. This is from the lower chakras, domination. The other one shows that people are close to each other and they have more understanding. This is from higher chakras. There is a lot of understanding between us. Therefore, there is no need for respect or consideration.

NIKA: Sometimes I feel I am a weak person and you have more respect for people that have power.

SHARAM: I am more considerate with people with more power. Why? Because when there is more power, it means there is a bigger ego and to overcome a big ego, I would have to become really tough. Why would I want to be tough all the time? Not much growth comes out of it, so it is not worth it. I work with them in different ways.

NIKA: I still have the conditioning that power is good.

SHARAM: Yes, you have to change that conditioning with understanding. You have to understand that a politician needs that power. He needs an army behind him. Or a teacher needs to have power so he can be effective. However, in relationships between people, if someone is bullying, deep inside they know there is no closeness with others. Bullies feel guilty and lonely. When someone has a lot of power and they bully others, the people who get close to them do so only because they like the bully's power and they like to submit to it. It is usually only one person, so the bully is close to one person and the rest of the world is their enemy.

NIKA: My nature is that I like to be with people, but I have a lot of conditioning that says I have to be powerful; otherwise I am no good.

SHARAM: That's why you have a fight inside. These two fight with each other all the time. That's why you asked your first question also *(Why do I respect people with power?)*. You have to see that your nature doesn't want what comes with power: bullying, guilt, loneliness. If you don't want the things that come with power, why would you want power itself?

THE PATH OF MEDITATION

CHRIS: My path has been meditation, but I am stuck in the mind more than anyone.

SHARAM: The *reason* your path is meditation is because your mind goes haywire. That is the *only* reason your path is meditation.

CHRIS: But meditation doesn't do anything for that. I'm still stuck in the mind.

SHARAM: Because meditation works gradually. It is a long path. The shortest path is to jump up and kiss everyone, dance with them, and be really happy…, to look at their eyes and say, "I love you *so* much," and *really* feel love. That is the shortest path. If you can't take the shortest path you have to take the longest path. It is very simple. Jump up and run and jump in the arms of Kate so her chair falls over. If you can do that, it is the shortest path. But with meditation it takes a while. Your path is meditation. You can't love.

I am impressed with how far you have come, but every day we have to start with where we are now. So more change is needed. But you can't do anything about it. You can't change. How can you change?

Take an injection called change? There is no such thing. It is gradual work for someone on the path of meditation. It is fast work for people who feel love. In love there is both meditation *and* love. They are combined. It becomes more powerful this way. Meditation is a steady uphill walking. It is very solid. Every step is solid. It is very good, but it is slower.

I DON'T GET IT

CHRIS: Sometimes I feel like I don't get it. Then I feel like a failure.

SHARAM: There are two ways of looking at failure. One is through comparison. In comparison to others, you feel like failure. Comparison is the way of the ego and it always pulls you down. The other way is when you feel negative. When you feel negative, you feel like a failure. You want to feel like a winner when you are negative? That is reserved for when you are positive. Right now you are in negativity. Of *course* you feel like a failure.

GOOD JOB

NIKA: In the past you have given me exercises that I have done, but I think they have not worked for me. Is that because I didn't do them very well?

SHARAM: The worst thing one can say is, "I did not do a good job; that's why it didn't work for me." The fact is that those exercises *have* done their job. There was so much ignorance back then, but now everything is more subtle. As much as you work, you see the results. Today you do your exercises with this new vision and understanding that you have. You do it with more totality because you have become more subtle. If you think that before you didn't do a good job, then you will be afraid that you won't be able to do a good job today either. It brings doubt in, and that doubt doesn't let you work deeper. When we do something with doubt, we can't be total in it. There is no such thing as a bad job. Everybody does their best according to where they are. When you grow and you become aware, it is not as visible as let's say, making a million dollars or getting an "A" on an exam, so you think you have not grown. Sometimes if someone from the past gets in touch with you, they can see your change.

NIKA: So I had a wrong understanding that those exercises I did haven't worked for me, and I *did think* they probably were not going to work for me now either. So that's not true? They have worked for me, and they will work for me again?

SHARAM: Yes.

NIKA: Because of the high standards that my parents have given me, just being on the path and not working feels like doing nothing and wasting my potential.

SHARAM: You are using these high standards and talents to work on yourself. This is the highest work on Earth.

DO NOTHING

SHARAM: Working on the self really means doing nothing. We constantly think that we have to do hard work—sit down and meditate or go to a cave. But really working on the self is doing nothing; just whatever you do, pay attention to it. Understanding and looking at ourselves *is* working. You really don't have to do anything. The fact that you are not working really is work in the mystical sense. You always forget that the spiritual world is 180 degrees different from the outside world. They say you have to work hard and meditate, but I don't say that. Just anything you do, do it with attention. Be with it. This is what I call work. Every time we talk and I catch your resistance, that is work.

MOTIVATION

MONA: I don't feel like going to work. I can't decide what I should do.

SHARAM: To do anything you have to have motivation. Like right now, talking to me is important to you and you are here. You come because every time you talk to me, you get to know yourself more. It is also fun and you can see the impact it has on your life. Making money is not that important for you, so you are not motivated to go to work.

MONA: How can I create motivation in myself? Because I have desire to do a lot of things; I have a lot of ideas.

SHARAM: Having desire alone is very weak. People who have big desires usually don't get anywhere. What they want is impossible to reach. It is not doable. The reason they can't reach them is that humans don't trust themselves. Even if they get to what they want, they think it was a miracle or good luck. They think a fairy has flown down from the sky and made it happen.

It is okay that right now you are lazy and you don't want to work. One day, when the motivation comes, you will do your job happily.

You won't be lazy. For example, let's say the job that you are doing right now pays you three hundred dollars. If someone offers you ten thousand dollars to do it, you will want to do it right away and do your best at it. You will be very motivated. So motivation happens when you have something that interests you. You can try to change a desire to motivation but deep inside, you believe it is not going to work. You believe you can't do it. Then again you lose interest and you don't want to do it.

Now we want to see why you don't have motivation. The reason is that the classes, sittings, and connection that we have are of such a high quality that two or three hundred dollars is not that interesting anymore. When you have high quality inside, it is hard to find something outside that can compare to that quality.

But you should also know that in the world outside, anyone who reached to higher levels, who succeeded, started small, but with persistence they eventually got to the higher levels.

MORNINGS, MIND, AND MEDITATION

RANDY: As soon as I wake up, my mind starts working like crazy. Why?

SHARAM: Because it has rested through the night and now is ready to work. You have to use your mind because of the nature of your work; your mind has been trained to work all the time. When you sleep, it rests. When you wake up, it goes to the other extreme and starts working. If you never used your mind during the day, when you woke up in the morning, you would feel so cool and at ease. Your mind would be at ease too.

RANDY: Now that I have to use my mind all the time, does it conflict with my path?

SHARAM: If you increase your meditation, it will be all right.

MY MOTHER'S APPROVAL

MAYA: Why do I need my mother's approval even though I know she has lots of wrong conditionings, even though I know that her conditionings are those of the world and not in favor of the soul?

SHARAM: Because we all have a child inside of us and that child always seeks her mother's approval. It is not only the mother's approval we seek. Deep inside we feel empty. That's why we want others' approval. Also Every time we get that approval, for a moment we feel satisfied, but then, in the next moment, that satisfaction is gone.

FEELING EMPTY

NIKA: I am not doing anything in my life right now because I don't want to fall into the vicious circle of having a goal and being busy all the time. I want to concentrate on working on myself, but sometimes I feel so empty, I can't bear it, so I was wondering if maybe I should do something with awareness to help me be more centered. What is your advice?

SHARAM: When you do something, anything, you immediately create a goal. You become serious, and you can't be aware anymore. If you want to do something with awareness, it should not be serious. Just do something with totality, like be very aware of your movements. If it becomes serious, it is not going to bring any awareness to you. The fact is, there *is* nothing in life, so that feeling empty *is* the truth. You are feeling the reality. People mostly commit suicide because they feel this emptiness. They have been taught that if you feel empty, it is horrible and you should die. If you look at the emptiness with positivity, you will see that it is beautiful. It is reality. All you have to do is concentrate on getting distance from the ego. It's very good that you are not doing anything right now, because anything you do just makes your ego bigger. You just have to look at your ego and see how you are attached to your mind.

NIKA: It's true. When I use my mind I enjoy it. Why is that?

SHARAM: Because they *(family and school)* have taught you all your life that this is the most important thing. Your family puts so much value on developing the mind and education that if you want to learn something, they will do anything to help you. But for other things, they don't care as much. It is very essential for you to understand that the mind is not going to take you anywhere. One can work hard for years and make a lot of money, and maybe, when they become older, they might want to understand something about themselves; but usually it's too late. People who start working on themselves at your age *(early twenties)* are the ones that become a help to people that did not do anything for themselves until old age. This is what I did. I worked on myself when I was your age and now I am helping people who are just learning that the path of mind has not worked for them.

NIKA: So when I feel empty, should I do something without a goal like painting? Or is it better to stay with that emptiness and maybe fall apart?

SHARAM: If you do something without a goal, when there is no getting a grade for it and there is no admiration of society for it, what happens is that you can become total with that work because there is no pressure. That totality makes the work extraordinary and unique. But knowing this may also create another goal *(to become total)*, and the ego becomes big again. The only people that have unique art are the ones that can keep the balance between wanting to do the art and not being attached to it. Also they aren't focused on making money from it. The person who wants to make money from it doesn't have real art. It is a waste of time. The best thing to do is to do something that is not admired by others like cleaning the floor or washing the dishes with awareness. With this kind of work, people don't say, "Wow you did such an amazing job washing those dishes." That's why in ashrams they give people these kinds of jobs to do, because it helps them be centered and at the same time there is nothing that the ego can boast about.

NIKA: But when I wash dishes, it doesn't fulfill me. I feel like something is missing. It's not fun.

SHARAM: It is the ego that is not fulfilled. We usually enjoy doing something that has a result because this is what society has taught us. You have to pay attention to wanting to do something for the results. What you really need is to do something without any goal. You will enjoy washing the dishes if you understand this concept that real enjoyment comes when you become one with whatever you are doing. Doing something with a goal is only food for the ego. The enjoyment that comes from that is always followed with misery. There is so much enjoyment in doing anything with awareness.

Totality can come only through acceptance.
If we accept totally
we will be total in whatever we do.

☙ SHARAM ❧

THE ILLUSION OF LACK

CHRIS: How do we look at our desire? For example, right now I have a desire to connect with you and get some deeper understanding.

SHARAM: Wait, let's look at the desire. You feel that you lack understanding. You feel that you lack connection. You want to do something with understanding and connection. Somebody wants to do something with money or a gadget. They are lacking money. Somebody desires friendship. All desiring comes from lacking something, which comes from feeling a lack inside; but there is no lack. It is all illusion, born from thinking, from the mind. Thinking becomes a wall and we can't see what is happening right now in the moment. We are in the mind where everything is illusion. The real is not what is in here *(point to his head)*. The real is something that is totally in the moment.

For example we think, "I lack connection because I feel like I'm not whole. I lack understanding because I feel like I don't understand. I need a little bit more understanding to become enlightened or to get somewhere." You see, all of a sudden this thing in the mind becomes something real on the outside that we think we need. "I feel like I'm not happy. I need that one gadget to become happy." It's just thinking. The nature of all of us is total happiness, total fulfillment, it is Existence, it is God. But the mind takes us to illusion, take us to the wrong place and then of course in illusion there is something lacking. What is lacking? The real! The real is lacking in the illusion, but we think a gadget or an understanding or a connection or friendship, a goal, or a million dollars is lacking. And when I get that million, then I see that I need two million. When somebody's going to give you money, you are happy because you are going to get the money. Then you get the money and you put it somewhere, in your drawer or in the bank, and it's like it doesn't exist anymore. How many times have you really worked hard to make some money? You were happy to get it. Now those times are past and you are still sitting here thinking you need more, but if you get more, it will be the same as last time. It just will not fulfill you.

Every week when I was a kid, there was a show on TV called "Millionaire" or something. Every week this man would go to someone's home and give them a million dollars as a gift. The show showed how people's lives got entangled and ruined by the money. Anybody who got a million dollars, their life got destroyed. One day the host of the show finally said, "Let's go and destroy another family." It's amazing. Unless you have wisdom, you just get destroyed.

RABIA: So if we're happy we do not desire?

SHARAM: Yeah—if you're really happy, you do not desire.

RABIA: So we just have to figure out how to be happy all the time.

SHARAM: No you don't have to figure it out because figuring it out means again, using the mind. If you try to figure it out with the mind, you never will, because no-desiring comes from no-mind.

MAYA: You mentioned the other day that happiness is very simple. You said, "If you are not miserable you are happy,"

SHARAM: Yes, that's very good. If you are not miserable, then you are happy. And what does that really mean? Not thinking. Slow down the thinking process. That's what meditation has done for you— it has slowed down the thinking process. You are all much happier than when I first met you.

BALANCING MONEY

NIKA: My male is comfortable with money. Money always comes to me and I don't worry about if I have enough or not, but my female is cheap. I spend money easily for things that I think are necessary, but for things that are not as necessary, I have a hard time spending. Is this being cheap?

SHARAM: This is not being cheap. If the male wants more money, it's usually to get cars and things to show how powerful he is, so he can dominate others. If the female wants more money, it is to buy more makeup, clothes, and things like that, which also is a subtle way of domination. If you are content with what you have, that's wonderful. What you explained about yourself is the sign of contentment. It shows that your male and female are healthy. They are more balanced.

BREAK IT TO MAKE IT

NIKA: I feel like since I cut myself off from the financial privileges I had with my family, my first chakra has gotten into trouble. I think I was fine before that. Is that true?

SHARAM: If the first chakra is strong and doesn't have blockages, it doesn't get into trouble. It doesn't become worse.

NIKA: So how come it seems like I am worse?

SHARAM: It is always like that: when you want to really grow, you break whatever exists and you start over. Imagine you are walking along a sidewalk, like a cobblestone sidewalk. In one part of the walkway, the bricks are broken, are ruined, but as you are passing them, you don't look down. When you go further, you do look down, but in this section of the walkway there is nothing wrong. All the bricks are intact. Now you go back a little bit and all of a sudden you see the part that was ruined and you say, "Oh, this walkway has become worse," but that is not true. The ruined part was there before. You just didn't see it then. Now you see it and you want to repair it. A lot of people have so much money, but they go toward drugs and alcohol to numb themselves. They go lower and lower until they hit the bottom. That's where they start growing, building themselves from nothing. There are also some people that suffer and they don't grow until they die.

NIKA: So anybody who wants to work on themselves, they have to go back to the first chakra and start from there?

SHARAM: Yes, most people have lots of problems in first chakra. They desire. They are not satisfied. But remember, we don't do anything. Existence does it all. It takes us back to where we need to work, and we start from there.

NIKA: So even if you have lots of money, you could have lots of problems in the first chakra?

SHARAM: The first chakra is not only about money. No matter how much money someone has, they will still feel like they don't have enough. The problem in the first chakra is desire. While you are getting money *(making or winning it, whatever)*, you are happy. As soon as you get a hold of some money, the moment you have it, it is over. It is almost like you don't have it. One is always hungry for more. If money could satisfy the hunger, the desire, rich people wouldn't run after money anymore. They might have billions of dollars, but inside they think they don't have enough. They have to make more. Right now, with understanding, you are repairing your first chakra.

NIKA: You have told me I am content. How does contentment fit into this?

SHARAM: It is true, you are content. However that contentment needs to grow. It is growing every day. You are a lot more content compared to a lot of people. If you become one hundred percent content, your first chakra will open up totally. However, you have to know that we don't want the first chakra to open totally all of a sudden, because we have to clean up the higher chakras more before we do that. If the first chakra opens up before we clean the higher ones, we can go crazy.

In fact, contentment means that your first chakra *is* clean, you have trust for Existence; if we don't trust, we don't come out of the first chakra.

NIKA: How do male and female energy fit into this?

SHARAM: The more balanced and healthy our male and female are, the more open the first chakra is and the more kundalini can come up. Kundulini awakens when balanced energy enters the first chakra. Then we enjoy our life.

APPRECIATION
JUST DO IT!

MELINA: How can we be appreciative?

SHARAM: Simply by appreciating. Saying thank you, being happy, not being sad, this is how we appreciate. Some people get so much, and still they think they have not gotten enough. Complaining is the opposite of appreciation. Being happy, being amazed, saying "wow," these are all appreciation.

THE FIRST CHAKRA

SHARAM: In the first chakra, you don't share anything. You are afraid of not having enough. You are always afraid. In the second chakra, you start sharing. How do you get from the first to the second? When you feel love *or* when you feel that there is enough, you don't worry anymore, and you go to the second chakra.

THE SECOND CHAKRA AND ITS DESIRE TO DOMINATE

SHARAM: The second chakra is female, so there is no power in it. When one is in the second chakra, they are power-obsessed. Therefore, the desire to dominate comes from the second chakra. When you gain power, you are not in the second chakra anymore, you come to the third. And in the third you want more and more power.

MAYA: Does that mean when we come to third chakra, we don't want to dominate?

SHARAM: In the second chakra because there is no power, there is more struggle for power. So the domination is not subtle. It is more like a temper tantrum. However, when you gain power, the domination becomes more subtle. It is more political.

LONELINESS

SHARAM: Loneliness belongs to the lower chakras. In the higher chakras there is no loneliness. That's why, in the lower chakras, we seek to feel unity all the time—because we feel lonely. We want to be with others all the time or we keep ourselves busy. When we go to the higher chakras there is no loneliness. One connects with the self mostly. That's why people go to monasteries when they get to the higher chakras.

Here we don't do that; we work on all our centers all the time.

YOU CAN'T FIX IT
IF YOU AIN'T GOT THE TOOLS

NIKA: Sometimes I have to be firm with people to keep things in order. I know if I'm not firm, chaos will happen and I will be miserable because of it. But when I am firm, I feel miserable too because I feel guilty for being tough on them. Why is that? What should I do?

SHARAM: The male gets tough, and the female regrets it. As long as we are on Earth, this is what happens. When you go deeper, you see that this whole dynamic comes from wanting to dominate. Domination is from the second chakra. If you want to fix this, you need to get out of where you are.

NIKA: Yes, that's what I want. But how do I do that?

SHARAM: In order to come out of a place where you are stuck, you have to use two things. The first is awareness and the second is understanding. You have to be constantly aware of things that are happening around that issue, in this case wanting to dominate, and bring more understanding to it.

NIKA: I understand you, but I feel bad that after all this time working on myself, I have to start working on a lower chakra. It feels like I am going backwards.

SHARAM: This is how it works: first you open and clean the higher chakras. Then you bring the awareness that you have gained from this work on the higher chakras and use it to clean your lower chakras. Without awareness, the lower chakras might get cleaned a little bit here and there, but the ultimate way of cleaning and opening them is to use awareness. Awareness comes from working on your higher chakras. So while you are working on yourself, you'll still have all the attributes of the lower chakras with you, except that now, because you have gained more awareness, every time you act from these lower chakras, you'll be better able to look at it.

Then with this higher awareness and higher understanding you will have the choice to either continue with these behaviors and feelings or stop them. The only time we don't have a choice and we fall into problems is when we don't have enough awareness.

In old times, when people were working on their higher chakras, they would go to monasteries because they didn't want to get pulled down by lower chakras. Today we work with balance. We work on all the chakras at the same time. So we don't need to go to a monastery.

ANGER

MELINA: What is anger?

SHARAM: Anger means I want to prove to you that I can overpower you. When I am angry at you, it means I want to dominate you. If you immediately surrender, my anger goes away. If you want to resist even a little bit, I get more angry. Therefore, anger just means that the person wants to show his or her power over the other person.

SEX AND THE CHAKRAS

SHARAM: If sex is only a physical relief, you only involve your first and second chakras. However, if the people are totally involved, then real sex happens. When love is there, then the fourth chakra is also involved. The fourth is the bridge between the three lower and the three upper chakras. That is why they call it making love, because the heart is at work. That is what I call real sex.

JEALOUSY

MELINA: What is jealousy?

SHARAM: Let's say someone is wearing a very nice outfit. You see it and get jealous. You say to yourself, consciously or not, "How dare she look so good!" Even if you have the same outfit you think, "How dare she buy something that I wear! She is below me." What happens here is that these thoughts bring you to your emotional body, the feeling body. Since the thoughts are negative, they hit the negative part of the emotional body and it starts projecting itself out as jealousy. You feel jealous.

On the other hand, if for some reason you go to your heart, like if you see an old friend that you like very much, because an open heart is positive, the reflection of heart on the emotional body is also positive. You experience a lot of good feelings. The same happens in the mental body, the thinking body, except instead of feelings, we experience positive thoughts. When we are in the heart, along with the positive feelings, we also experience positive thoughts. So according to which chakra we are in, we have different feelings and thoughts.

We are learning about our chakras. But we don't even have to call them chakras because people associate chakras with Eastern mysticism. We don't want to subscribe to any labels. We should just call them centers of our soul. Each one of them has a certain function, and learning about their functions brings a lot of understanding into our lives.

*Jealousy means that your heart is closed.
If your heart was open,
you would not be jealous.*

❧ SHARAM ☙

A MYSTIC'S JOB

SHARAM: The heart chakra is the center where the higher and lower chakras meet each other. That's why, when you are in your heart, there is the possibility of falling down to the lower chakras at any moment. That is why love is so fragile. You cannot stay in the heart for a long time at this point in your growth; eventually you will fall. That's why when two people meet and fall in love with each other, in the beginning everything is so high, they don't think about sex at first. If they think about sex in the beginning, then it is not love. That is lust. But when real love happens, you don't think about sex for a while. Later you start thinking about sex. When this happens, you have fallen from the heart to the lower centers. And when there is sex, it is very hard, if not impossible, to go high anymore. There will be lots of fight and struggle and problems. What does a mystic do? A mystic's job is to bring people to their heart and to the higher centers. With a mystic you come to your heart and you start having fun, but then again you fall down and you have problems, and again the mystic comes and takes you higher.

MONEY, WORK, AND A BIG EGO

AL: You mentioned that I am working on my fifth chakra, but I feel my ego is bigger now. How does that work?

SHARAM: When the fifth chakra becomes stronger, the ego gets bigger and bigger. It is getting ready for its own explosion, its own destruction. The fifth chakra is the peak of the ego. The first chakra doesn't have any ego. The second chakra has a small ego. The third chakra has a bigger ego; it's strong. Being in the heart, the fourth chakra, is very sweet because that is where real understanding comes and love happens. It's so sweet that we have to remember to keep moving or we'll get stuck there. In the fifth chakra the ego becomes very strong so that you can see it. It's not small. We can't see a small ego; it is hard. Also, this chakra usually relates directly to money. With money, a person gets power. They feel that they have prestige. Usually a person in the fifth chakra gets a lot of attention; other people listen to them. So money, work, and a big ego are all related to this fifth chakra. Actually the first five chakras all relate to money from their own perspective. For example, in the first chakra money is for survival.

DREAMS AND CHAKRAS

LEILA: When we dream, which chakra are we in?

SHARAM: Dreams take different forms in different chakras; each has its own quality. For example, if you are having sex and then you sleep and you are in the second chakra, your dreams will relate to that. Another example is that you are running around and working from morning 'til night; then you are sleeping in the first chakra. You'll dream of work or running around. If you are angry at someone and you sleep, you are sleeping in the third chakra. If you are in your heart and you feel love and you sleep, then you are sleeping in the fourth chakra. Each of them has dreams with its own qualities. When you are meditating here and you fall asleep, you are sleeping in the fifth and sixth chakras. When you fall asleep, you go to a different world.

ENLIGHTENMENT IS EASY

TOM: When people use drugs, their ego steps aside, they come to the moment, and they can enjoy. How come the ego can go away so easily with drugs, but here we try so hard and we can't do it?

SHARAM: When they use drugs, it gives them all that momentarily, but they get addicted to it. Then, they have to use more and more all the time. I say, it's not hard at all to put your ego aside. Unity with Existence is very easy, but the mind is very complex and always wants to go after complexity. That's why it misses such an easy thing. It makes it seem hard. The only reason we cannot do it is because it's so easy. If I had asked you to go to the top of Mt. Everest, you would have done it by now. Enlightenment, being in the moment, understanding everything deeper, and being clear—they all are very easy. The only thing that drugs do is to stop the mind, and because the mind has stopped, you get to see how easy it really is. Usually, when you are doing drugs, you are lazy and you don't want to do anything hard. Therefore, you just see the easy. The mind doesn't have a chance to bring the complexity in.

*Existence is all fun—
the mind is no fun at all.*

∽ SHARAM ∽

THE GREAT OPPORTUNITY

RABIA: When I drink tea with awareness, my mind still goes everywhere.

SHARAM: The mind can go anywhere. It's good. It gives us an opportunity to watch it. When you are sitting and meditating, this is your homework, to just sit back and watch the mind. If you find yourself attached to the thinking, that's fine; just go back to watching. All of this is part of the process of growth. Existence always gives us the opportunities we need.

MIND
THE GREAT DEFENDER

Sharam was looking at Debby for a long time. At one point, he began asking other people what their reaction was to him looking at Debby for such a long time. After some people shared, he came back and asked Debby what was going on for her.

DEBBY: I was tense and wound up when you first began looking at me. After a while, I started to relax and began to breathe more deeply, but it was taking time. When you asked everyone to share, I started thinking and that relaxation that was happening stopped.

SHARAM: Your let-go was conditional. If people talk you can't let go. If they don't talk, you have peace and silence and you can let go. Maybe you started thinking because my focus was not totally on you anymore; you were not getting my full attention?

DEBBY: Yes. I felt like I needed all of your attention to reach deep relaxation. So by thinking, am I defending myself?

SHARAM: You become defensive when you start thinking. There was something you didn't like, so you closed yourself by thinking. Really, the bottom line of thinking is to defend oneself. The whole job of the mind is to defend the self. Even distinguishing between a marshmallow and a pillow, we have to distinguish in order not to eat the pillow (lots of laughter). If the mind is not there, we sleep on marshmallows and eat the pillow. Even the job of distinguishing things, which is the main job of the mind, even that is for defending the self. Otherwise you end up eating the pillow. Why do we need to defend? Because we are scared, we are afraid something might happen to us we don't like.

DEBBY: So I started thinking, because I couldn't express what I needed? I wasn't aware what I needed?

SHARAM: Yes, your awareness came later, which is fine. So many people on Earth, they never become aware. Your awareness now, came a few minutes later. Very soon it will be right away.

So one more time—I was looking at you and then I asked people what they were feeling. When they started talking, you started thinking. The mind came in to think, but really it came to defend itself from something it didn't like; it wanted my full attention.

CUNNING MIND

SHARAM: One of the things the mind does is to take something I said before and use it somewhere else completely out of context. At the time and in relation to the situation I said it, it had meaning and was beautiful; but used out of context, it becomes horrible. When the mind uses something out of context, first it means that it has memorized it *(a deeper understanding was missing)* and secondly, it is using what has been said with a lot of condemnation. The mind picks out the negative and forgets about the positive.

The mind is very cunning. It changes things. It makes them smaller or bigger to serve its own purposes. Just now you saw the system of ego, the way it operates. You told me earlier that you were upset because you don't see any growth in yourself. As we talked, at one point you said, "It is a miracle that I have so much patience now, because my mother didn't have patience for anything." Then I reminded you that this is a big change in you. So don't say you have not grown. This is the growth you were looking for, but then you said, "Big deal, I have patience compared to my mother who has none." See how the mind makes the positive small and the negative big or vice versa? All to fit its agenda. The reality is that there are no problems in Existence; it is only the mind making them up or making problems where they don't exist. Everything is perfect.

NIKA: So I have grown some but my mind doesn't let me see it. Is that right?

SHARAM: Yes, that's the truth. Mind sometimes lets you see and sometimes doesn't let you see. Sometimes it makes something big and sometimes it makes the same thing small. That's why it won't let you hear when someone tells you, you haven't grown at all. Instead of hearing what they have said, you all of a sudden start telling them how much you *have* grown. You tell them they don't understand; you defend yourself. And if someone tells you you have grown a lot, you will say, "No way, I haven't grown at all." The mind does everything in its benefit. What is the benefit of the mind? Just to prove its point. It wants to prove that what "I" *(it)* said is right. It uses everything it can to prove that it is right, including making things big and small. It doesn't matter what it is trying to prove, it just wants to prove it is right. Why, because if it is right, then the ego becomes big and important.

This happens in both subtle ways and gross ways. For example, you have grown in some areas and you haven't grown in other areas. So if you say I haven't grown, it is true, and if you say I have grown, it is also true. Things that are in the gray area, more subtle, the mind takes hold of them and makes them small or big for its own advantage. But if I say I bought six newspapers yesterday and somebody responds, "Hey, why are you lying: you only bought one newspaper," this is gross *(more obvious)*. The mind is still doing the same thing—making things big: I bought six newspapers—but it is easier to detect. Not only that, but the mind pulls all these tricks and we fall for them. We say, "Oh, I have not grown at all," and then we cry and feel bad or the opposite, "I have grown a lot," and we feel important and puffed up. The emotional body is suffering a lot from the tricks of the mind.

NIKA: So does that mean that there is no problem in the emotional body and the only reason we fall apart is because of the mind's tricks?

SHARAM: Yes, exactly.

NIKA: It feels like we fall apart more when we repress?

SHARAM: Repression means pressure. It means pressing on the emotional body. Earlier, when we talked, you said, "I have not grown at all." This is pressure on the emotional body, and when you said that you cried. Remember? How do we create this pressure? With negative thoughts. These negative thoughts are like a fishing hook that is cast into the emotional body and hooks into a related negative emotion and pulls it out to the conscious mind. Then you start suffering.

GIVING SPACE

NIKA: I have a problem when people make a big deal out of nothing. I think they are being spoiled.

SHARAM: Everyone operates according to their own capacity: something that is big for them is small for the next person. Something that is a life and death situation for one person could seem like just being spoiled for you and something that is big for you could seem like being spoiled for them. We cannot say what is being spoiled and what is not. That is not giving space to others. That is why I work with every tiny thing that people have and don't consider it as being spoiled. Everyone has a certain capacity. If you understand this, your love grows. Otherwise, your heart is closed and you are judging all the time.

NIKA: Now I see that because my mother was very tough, and she was so careful that we didn't become spoiled, when I see others getting upset with simple things, I think they are spoiled.

SHARAM: Yes, your mother helped you to have more capacity, she didn't coddle you. You have to understand that other people have different capacities.

*I give space for people to go high and low.
The only thing I do is to give space.*

∽ SHARAM ∽

BLOWING THINGS OUT OF PROPORTION

MAYA: For a long period of my life, I was put down and repressed by people around me. Why was that?

SHARAM: This problem of getting repressed or put down happens to almost everyone. You always see it in movies: some big kid bullies a little kid. But the big kid also gets bullied by some other big kid or his dad. Some people get put down by their parents. So everyone goes through this in some way. In your case, because of the way you are, having a small body, you blow everything out of proportion. You see everything bigger than it is.

MAYA: But it is not only that I see things bigger. I make them bigger. I create something so big that even other people see it as big.

SHARAM: You just put your finger on the main point. What is the point? The main point is that seeing is the same as doing. How we see something is just as important as what really happened. Seeing is just as important. If you see something as big, you think of it as big, it becomes big.

MAYA: But it seems like instead of making things big, I have made things small. For example, I was treated in a way that I didn't like, but instead of expressing myself and making a case out of it, I made it small and tried to ignore it. So by and by, I became more repressed.

SHARAM: Blowing things out of proportion means you make things bigger, or you make them smaller. This is so interesting. For years, anything you didn't like, because you were not able to express yourself, you made it smaller, so you could ignore it. And you know, expressing is not just talking about something; you have to be in touch with your emotions, and also you have to be able to deal with them in a positive manner. In this way, expressing can help you grow. With you, every time any emotions came up, you would either fall apart or you would try to push them back down, because you were always very uncomfortable with emotions. You couldn't tolerate being emotional. That means you were male even though you are a woman.

MAYA: Why couldn't I tolerate emotions?

SHARAM: When you are very serious, you don't accept emotions. When you got emotional growing up, they told you, "What is this, snap out of it, be rational." This is how the door to your emotions was closed, so you could not tolerate any emotions anymore because you thought of emotions as bad.

SPILLED MILK

RANDY: Recently you've talked about resistance a lot. It has caused me to watch it more. At work, for example, a customer comes and starts lying to me. I see that he is a cheat right away and my resistance comes up. I don't reject him; I work with him, but the resistance is there. This causes me to feel unsatisfied and unhappy.

SHARAM: There is an old proverb about this. We call it a cow with gallons of milk. Every day, this cow gives lots and lots of milk, but every day, at the end of its milking, she kicks the bucket over and spills all the milk. She is a good cow; she does a good job, but in the end, she ruins it. You are like that. You give service to this customer, but you are not satisfied. Either don't give service, or if you do, do it with total freedom and satisfaction, without any resistance. The reason you resist is because you look at the situation with your mind and mind doesn't accept whatever it thinks is wrong or whatever it doesn't like. If you go with your heart, there will be no resistance.

FARIN: What do you mean by going with the heart? In a situation like this, where we see this person is trying to cheat us, how can we go with the heart?

SHARAM: This person has been sent by Existence. This is a test. Existence is testing you to see how free you are. And remember, if we are hard on others, we will be hard on ourselves too. We won't have freedom. Existence is creating everything, and everything is an opportunity for us.

RANDY: So this is a problem of being in the mind?

SHARAM: Yes, the mind always wants everything to be fair and exact and according to rules.

RANDY: I guess the only solution is to do more meditation and become more aware.

SHARAM: Yes, and understanding. Understanding is the coming together of the mind and the heart. You have told me that you forget what I have said in a couple of hours; you forget what you have understood. But if understanding happens deeply, you won't need to remember it. Remembering happens through the mind, remembering means thoughts, therefore if you forget, that's even better, because if we only learn through the mind, everything will be shallow.

But we can use the mind for understanding things more deeply. Understanding is the path for this century, because our minds work a lot. In old times, people wouldn't use their mind that much. Most things were based on trust. Today trust doesn't have any meaning—we have to understand things. This is the century of mind. It is interesting that two hundred years ago, there wasn't much understanding. People lived through their instinct. Understanding belonged to people who would grow so high and would become enlightened. But today, since there is little trust, we have to understand to grow; we have to use the mind to connect with the soul. The heart and mind have to come together. It is hard, but trusting is hard too. Imagine without understanding, you have to take everything on faith and trust. As a matter of fact understanding is easier than trusting blindly.

With understanding we can change things. For example, negativity exists on the surface. If we bring understanding to a negative situation, we will go deeper and then the negativity disappears. When I talk about some negative emotions, like anger, people here like it because they want to understand it more deeply. They know that with deeper understanding, they won't get angry anymore. Deeper understanding takes us deep into our soul. We come off the surface. On the surface everything is negative. Mind means the surface—shallow. Only understanding takes us to our heart, takes us to the layers of our soul. The heart is the center of our soul.

Now you see that when someone shows up and is lying to you, this is a test from Existence, to get you off the surface and into the depths.

FORGET IT!

SHARAM: If you forget things, it shows that you are in the heart, in the moment; because memory is of the past.

MY OWN CREATION

NIKA: I see, more and more, that everything is my fault.

SHARAM: There are three groups of people. The first group is the ones that don't have any understanding. They think, "I am the best and everybody else is at fault." The second group has a little more understanding. They say, "Well, I have problems, but everybody else has them too, so I'm fine." The third group has higher understanding. They see that everything is their own creation, that there *is* nobody else. When you become enlightened, you go beyond even this. You see that there is no fault; you are one with everyone. Then you can help others see how *they* create everything around them.

*Resistance means that we forget that we are
creating everything in our lives,
and we start blaming others for our problems.
This is a subtle way of resisting.
Today we are working on the subtleties
of understanding resistance.
There is more room for me
to tell you about your egos.*

∽ SHARAM ∽

BLAME

SHARAM: If there is a problem in your life, you blame it on others. You think it is someone else's fault. This is where you go wrong. Even if it *looks* like it is someone else's fault, it just appears that way. It really is not. As long as you blame it on other people, Existence knows you are not ready to be taught the lesson of it. It won't teach a higher lesson to you. Existence won't share understanding with you, because it knows you are not ready. It will not give you any higher understanding. The moment you take the situation as your own fault, all of a sudden Existence comes up with a lesson that is exactly for you. This never fails.

Existence will give you such amazing understanding, so profound, so deep. The day you really see that in any situation, *you* are responsible, *you* are at fault, *not* the other person, you become free.

BLAME ME, PLEASE

SHARAM: If people get blamed by others it is only because it makes them suffer, and suffering cleanses their karma. If in interactions with people, you do something wrong, and they blame you, you make more karma than you get rid of, because you created this situation and you need this karma to grow from it. But if you get blamed for something you haven't done, your karma will get cleansed.

NIKA: So basically people are helping us to clean our karma by blaming us?

SHARAM: Yes, exactly. So we see again that Existence is impeccable.

THE ETERNAL LIGHTNESS OF NASTINESS

SARAH: I have been nice to some people, but they have been nasty to me. It breaks my heart. Why is that?

SHARAM: There are two parts to everything that happens. The way it looks on the outside and what is really happening at a deeper level. When we look at a situation, we see the outside, which might be ugly, but the inside is completely the opposite; it is very beautiful. *(The opposite is also possible—the outside is nice and the inside is ugly.)* We usually look at everything superficially. This is what is happening right now. You are looking at the surface and it is ugly, but if you look deeper, you will see so much love of Existence in there. How else can Existence help you to clean your karma and become lighter? Existence has a karma balance sheet for everyone. If you do something nice for someone and they are nice back, you balance the karma on Existence's sheet between the two of you. But if they don't repay you, then your account will be balanced by Existence. It takes some of your karma and gives it to that person: you become lighter and they become heavier. The reason you feel hurt is that, when the karma is leaving, we feel pain and hurt. So even if you understand the concept, still you will feel the hurt, because the karma is leaving. Creating karma and getting rid of it, both feel the same.

WHAT GOES AROUND COMES AROUND
A COMPLICATED MATTER

JESSE: People hurt me a lot. I don't understand why?

SHARAM: We create everything. We do something and in response people hurt us. If you are mature enough, you won't create that anymore. There is a law in Existence that no one can hurt us without a reason. There are only two possibilities. One is that you might have hurt someone in your past lifetimes or earlier in this lifetime. Now, that person is hurting you to clean your karma. You might start thinking, "Well, if I hurt this person in a past lifetime, they must have hurt me first in some lifetime before that, so where does all this hurting start?" It could have started with someone hurting you without intending to. Maybe they were boasting or bragging about something and you didn't like it, and this whole chain reaction got started. We got hurt because we lacked some understanding of the situation. They didn't try to hurt us, but because of this lack of understanding, something in us got hurt, so again it started with us. Or you do something unconsciously to hurt someone and they react. Because you don't know what you have done, you get hurt, thinking that they are hurting you for no reason. We have to remember that everything starts with us.

RESISTANCE AND FIGHT

SHARAM: Resistance creates the energy of fight and struggle in the air around us. When we resist, then fights and arguments happen, because that energy of fight has spread around the space. In general resistance means fight. You could be resisting one thing and the fight might be about something else, but as long as you are resisting, some sort of fight will be there.

YOU CAN STOP THEIR ANGER

MAYA: Why do people sometimes say things with anger and frustration?

SHARAM: Because they feel an energy of resistance in us and the only way they can express themselves is to say whatever it is with anger and pressure. In fact, this pressure is not to put down or push us away, it is only there to break our resistance. So when we resist, we make the other person say something with anger. It starts with our resistance. If we don't resist, the other person will not have any anger.

MAYA: What if we resist because someone is attacking us?

SHARAM: Anything that we don't like and want to hide in our unconscious, when it gets touched, it feels like an attack. Someone has said something to us and that thing has hit our weak point or a wound in us, and it feels like an attack. But no one can attack us. People put their finger on our wound and we resist—then they attack.

MAYA: What if there is no wound and somebody just puts their negativity on us?

SHARAM: If there is no wound, there would be no problem. Their negativity cannot happen unless we resist because of a wound in us.

MAYA: What if the person talking to us has a wound and puts the negativity of his wound on us?

SHARAM: It doesn't make any difference. If you don't have a wound, you won't get upset. The only time you get upset is when you have a similar wound. We are here to look at these wounds.

THE SECRET OF LOVE

MAYA: When I feel bad, people around me reject me immediately, and I feel hurt. Why is that?

SHARAM: This is the love of Existence. If they don't reject you, you get used to the bad mood and you will be miserable all the time. This way, Existence is pushing you to get out of it.

MAYA: But how do I get out of it? Isn't this repressing it, trying to get out of it?

SHARAM: No, it is not, because you work with it. You don't want to feel rejected. Start by breathing deep and exhaling with force out of your mouth for few minutes. This helps to get rid of some karma and pressure. Of course, you should look deeper and bring understanding in by talking to me, either right away or later on.

MAYA: I understand all this, but I still feel hurt in my heart, because it feels like there is no love out there.

SHARAM: This is why I always say that love has to come from inside because outside of us are people with limitations. In fact, love is the space and capacity that we have inside of us. Some people have more, some people have less. Basically, the foundation of this space and capacity is understanding. The more you understand everything and everyone deeper, the more love you have for them.

MAYA: How does the understanding come?

SHARAM: The female feels; the male expresses and has reasoning. When these two come together, understanding happens. So the stronger your male and female become, and the more they balance, the more you understand. If there is more male and less female, the male eats the female all up, and we become aggressive. If there is more female and less male, the female overpowers the male, and we become passive. Equal amounts of both transform us to a higher level.

MAYA: So basically people give love to us based on the capacity of their inner vastness and understanding.

SHARAM: Exactly.

MAYA: I feel much better because now I know everybody is doing their best and instead of looking for love outside, I should focus on opening more space inside of me with understanding. I should work on my own inner vastness and bringing my own love out.

SHARAM: Yes, that's the spirit.

*Bridging with the inside brings joy.
Bridging with the outside often
brings irritation or rejection.*

∽ SHARAM ∽

BEAUTY AND THE BEAST

KATE: When I resist it's really bad. Everybody hates it. Why is that?

SHARAM: When you are more real, your resistance is more visible. The opposite is also true, your non-resisting *(acceptance or let-go)* is also more visible. That's why when someone is real and is not resisting, you like to be near them, because when they don't resist, it's easy to see and you like it. Those who hide their resistance more, people want to stay away from, because they don't have that not resisting part. They resist all the time. So, people that are more real, when they are negative—yes—everybody hates it, but when they become positive, people really like them.

THE SUBTLE LOVE OF EXISTENCE

KATE: When my husband falls into negativity, he pushes me away. Why is that?

SHARAM: Existence has a mechanism that when someone becomes unaware and falls into negativity, they start pushing away people around them. It could be in the form of fight or of just being closed. This is the love of Existence. Existence wants people to stay away from someone who is not feeling good. This is the wisdom of Existence. People do it in different ways. Someone that is more advanced would say, "Let's not see each other today." Someone else just hides behind their computer, or finds some other way to push everyone away. All they are saying is, "I am unaware and I don't want to disturb you." You see there is so much love in subtleties.

FREE INSIDE AND OUT

FARIN: Sometimes, when my boyfriend and I have a plan to do something, I suggest we do something else. Randy feels that I take his freedom away when I do this. I want to understand this: how do I take his freedom away?

SHARAM: If someone *can* take our freedom away, he should do it. If one is capable of taking our freedom away, so be it. It is better to do it, because if our freedom depends on others and can be taken away, then it is not freedom. Freedom comes from inside. The only freedom is inner freedom. What is inner freedom? It means whatever is happening is okay. The one who complains about his freedom being taken away shows that he has a knot inside, a blockage. We have wrong information about freedom. Nobody can take anybody's freedom away. If you are able to do that, it simply shows that there was no freedom. Inner freedom comes from acceptance. Even if you are in jail, if you have acceptance, that prison will be like heaven for you. That is freedom, not what we have been taught. We have imprisoned ourselves on the inside, and we project it outside. So if we want to have freedom, we should know that it comes from inside, not from outside. If someone can take it away, let them, because real freedom cannot be taken away.

The other day I bought a rock. I paid one hundred dollars for it, but I hadn't left the store yet. I saw another rock which was worth six hundred dollars, and I liked it better, so I told the owner I wanted to buy that one instead and I would pay the five hundred dollar difference. He panicked, and said, "Oh, you changed your mind?" He told his wife, "This person changes his mind all the time." I said, "But by changing my mind, I'm paying you five hundred dollars more. Why do you get upset? My changing mind is in your benefit. It just made you more money." But he was complaining: "No, you always change your mind. You always do that." This I call not having freedom.

GET OUT YOUR FLY SWATTERS AND LET'S GO A-SWATTIN'

MONA: So many things seem to go wrong for me and I am worried about the future all the time. I don't know what to do.

SHARAM: When there is tension and chaos inside and there is no trust, everything goes wrong outside. When we struggle inside all the time, we project that outside of us. Everything we see outside is like a movie screen. It is all a projection of our inside. If we are worried about the future, not only will nothing go right now, but we will ruin the future also. You punish yourself all the time. Some tiny thing happens and your unconscious punishes you. Some tiny wrong thing inside brings big destruction outside. It is like a fly that is sitting on a projector in a movie theater. It is only a fly, but it makes a huge impression on the movie screen.

If you get confused inside, you fall apart and things start going wrong from there. Then, you think that you have done something wrong or someone else has done something wrong and you get upset and start to defend yourself. Instead of trusting that when something goes wrong on the outside it is just a sign that something is wrong on the inside, you get upset and you defend yourself. You just have to find out what the issue is on the inside and work on it; then, the next time something similar happens on the outside, you will recognize it as that issue; you will pay attention and not fall into the same trap. Not only should you not be upset, but you should be very happy to learn about yourself. Then everything will be wonderful.

We should also know that when there is misery, happiness is going to follow. This is a cycle. When misery is there, say to yourself, "It's okay, this is going to pass." That way you become detached from the misery and you jump to the positive. You bring the positive up; the negative automatically goes away. Detachment works like an eraser. It cleanses your unconscious; it changes your unconscious to conscious. If you do this a few times, the negative will say, "I better stay out of here. There is no room for me."

A WAKE UP CALL

MONA: How does my selfishness fit into all this?

SHARAM: What does it mean to be selfish? It means that you only think of yourself. You only do what *you* like to do and what is in your benefit. You don't consider anyone else. Every time you become unaware, you become very selfish. There are two parts in our unconscious, one is the higher self and the other is the lower self. The higher self is the one who punishes the lower self. The higher self wants to become awakened, so when you do something you don't like, like when you become selfish, somehow later you will punish yourself as a wake up call. There is another part of you which is your conscious mind, and it is very nice and kind and it thinks of others. The sum of all these is your life. When you are more loving, you are more conscious; when you are more selfish, you are less conscious. When worrying and selfishness come out of you, you have become unaware and negative. It makes you upset and you go to your emotions *(emotional body)* and you cry. Becoming emotional reinforces the negative. If you can detach yourself from that unhappiness, by and by the selfishness will get cleaned, because when you become detached from unhappiness *(the negative)*, you jump to the positive and there is no selfishness in the positive. You get used to staying in the positive. Then your life will start working.

GUILT BUSTER

AL: Every time I get into argument with someone, somehow I hurt myself. Why is that?

SHARAM: Because you feel guilty and your unconscious creates a situation where you get hurt. This is how you punish yourself.

AL: How can I stop that?

SHARAM: There *is* a way to get rid of the guilt. Every time you get into an argument or fight, afterward, sit down, either with that person or alone, and look at it deeper. See what the higher reason for this argument was. Look for the positive things that have come out of it. Bring a deep understanding to why Existence wanted this. If you find that deep understanding, you won't feel guilty and punish yourself anymore. Punishment means that we don't understand and we feel guilty. Feeling guilty is only a lack of understanding. You think it's your fault. You bring yourself (*your ego*) in. In fact, feeling guilty is thinking that you are a big shot. You think you are God, but you have done something bad, and now you have to punish yourself. If you know that Existence is in charge of everything, you won't feel guilty anymore, and you won't punish yourself anymore. It is very simple.

LET EXISTENCE BE YOUR JUDGE

MELINA: Sometimes when I say something, I don't know if what I said was okay or not and I get worried; then I do something where I hurt myself. For example, all of a sudden I see that I have scratched my arm so much that it hurts. Why do I do that?

SHARAM: Because you are a very good girl. So if you think you have hurt someone, you want to punish yourself. But being good is not enough. You have to go beyond it. Good is better than bad, right?! But you still have to go beyond it. Good is better than bad, but beyond is better than good.

MELINA: How do I go beyond it?

SHARAM: With understanding. You think this person is hurt because you said something and you wonder why you said it. "How could I have said such a thing?" Maybe they needed it. Without a doubt, every time someone gets hurt, in some way they needed it; it is good for them. But, you shouldn't do it intentionally, and you don't, you have good intentions. If you hurt someone, instead of punishing yourself, just go to them and talk about it. If they are not there, talk to me. If you punish yourself, you are saying, "I know better than Existence. I have to punish myself." This is very egoistic. In Existence there is no punishment. You might suffer to clean your karmas, but even that, your soul is creating. For example, someone has been unfair in some way and they get into an accident.

For you because you are fair, you want to punish yourself. The only reason you punish yourself is because your mind comes in and judges you. Don't let your mind be the judge, let me be your judge. If you talk with me, you will see there is no room for punishment in Existence. Existence never wants to punish us; it just wants to remind us of something or make us aware of something. It wants to teach us something. Existence is not about punishment. Existence is all love. Your mind wants to punish you; it doesn't want you to learn anything. The mind is a judge and a very harsh one. Anytime you want to hurt yourself, just stop and say, "I don't want the mind to be my judge; I want Existence to be my judge."

FROM NOWHERE TO NOWHERE

DEBBY: My life is complicated lately, absolutely overwhelming. There is so much I need to take care of everyday. What's going on?

SHARAM: You are feeling guilty about something. Tell me what you are punishing yourself for. You can easily simplify your life, but you have made it very complicated and now you are feeling that you are a victim of the life you created. This is a victim mentality, but really you are punishing yourself. Anyone who makes their life complicated in a subtle way is punishing himself. So why are you punishing yourself? Why are you making your life complicated?

DEBBY: When my Mom died and left me all that money, I was irresponsible with it and gave it all away. Now my husband has to work so hard and I feel guilty about that.

SHARAM: If you don't think that you were irresponsible, if you change this mentality of "I was irresponsible; my husband should not be working this much; if I wouldn't have given that money away...."

If you throw that out of the window because now it is useless to even think about it and instead just say, "The money I gave away to everyone was really their money." Then, it's fine. It needed to go. It came and went. If you don't feel bad about it, all of a sudden you have so much energy, ten thousand energies, to go towards making fresh money. It's amazing.

DEBBY: Wrong thinking.

SHARAM: Wrong thinking, yes, not wrong doing. What you did was perfect. Existence wanted you to give that money away and you did. Money came from nowhere and it went to nowhere. From nowhere to nowhere—it was perfect! When you don't look at it this way, you waste all that beautiful energy. Even unconsciously, when you think about it, you are throwing your energy away. That's why your life becomes complicated, heavy. Heavy means I don't have much energy.

DEBBY: Yes, kundalini goes away. There's no appreciation or acceptance and I become a victim thinking, "Why is this happening to me?"

SHARAM: Now, with this new look, you collect ten thousand energies and with this fresh energy, you can do amazing stuff. Just tell yourself that you have ten thousand fresh energies available, and with that energy—you're set. You're good to go. You're set for handling everything very smoothly.

BALANCE IS A MOMENT-TO-MOMENT THING

SHARAM: I want to open something with you Debby. You had this issue, this problem, whatever it was, and you didn't share. You were just sitting on it. I want to address this. When this happens, when you sit on something and don't open it, it shows that the female part has become strong. This is a characteristic of the female.

DEBBY: Isn't this unbalanced?

SHARAM: It's not, really. We have worked to make your female strong; at the same time you do have the male anytime you want to use it. A passive person does not have the male unless they get angry. Then their male comes up and they become aggressive. With you though, Debby, you have the male anytime you want to use it. You don't have to go to anger to get the male. You just make a decision and you bring the male in. Balance is a moment to moment thing. Total balance only happens when you are enlightened. Before enlightenment, the balance comes anytime you create it: when you are happy. When things become complicated, then the balance cannot happen like in this situation, you lost your energy by thinking, "Damn, I gave all that money away." Balance needs energy. If you don't waste your energy, then you can easily create balance between the male that you have had and the nice female that you have now. Your face, your hair have become beautiful. Before they were more male. Now they are more balanced, male and female, and you are beautiful because of the female we've been working on and have made strong. So for now, balance is a moment to moment thing. If you become clear, you become happy, and all of a sudden the male and female balance each other—they merge, become one, and in that moment, you are ecstatic. When you become enlightened, you will always be balanced.

TRICKS OF THE NEGATIVE MIND

KATE: I am unhappy and it seems like everything is the same, that nothing has changed, and I have not grown.

SHARAM: Negativity is always the same. Why doesn't it change? Because negativity is an illusion, and an illusion doesn't grow. Only positivity and beyond grows. That's why when we are in positivity everything is new, wonderful, and exciting. Growth is for real things like love, compassion, and understanding. An illusion is not real so it doesn't grow; the negative doesn't change. When your heart closes and you fall into negativity, you actually fall into an illusion that is just like it was before and will always be. Then you think you have not grown. Of course in negativity no one grows. Negativity cannot grow.

BREAKING FAITH

MELINA: I am worried because you told me you have a lot of faith in me. What if I do something to break that faith?

SHARAM: Always go with whatever comes up in the moment. If you bring in fear for the future—like, "What if I do something wrong and I break Sharam's faith, what if he doesn't like me anymore?"—this fear ruins the moment. Whatever happens in the moment, just go with that, and know that Existence is doing it. And trust that it's okay if people get angry with you. Just know that even that is necessary and that you can get past it. When you trust, you bring acceptance, even for negativity. Then you get courage to encounter hard situations.

There is nothing more exciting than love.
If we think of some things other than love,
they are also exciting
because our heart center is touched through them.
So as they say,
"Location, location, location"
for buying a house,
I say, "Love, love, love"
for having a good and full life.

∽ SHARAM ∽

www.ingramcontent.com/pod-product-compliance
Lightning Source LLC
Chambersburg PA
CBHW061256110426
42742CB00012BA/1935